Peace: A Very Short Introduction

VERY SHORT INTRODUCTIONS are for anyone wanting a stimulating and accessible way in to a new subject. They are written by experts, and have been translated into more than 40 different languages.

The Series began in 1995, and now covers a wide variety of topics in every discipline. The VSI library now contains over 350 volumes—a Very Short Introduction to everything from Psychology and Philosophy of Science to American History and Relativity—and continues to grow in every subject area.

Very Short Introductions available now:

Available soon:

For more information visit our website

www.oup.com/vsi/

Oliver P. Richmond

# PEACE

## A Very Short Introduction

OXFORD
UNIVERSITY PRESS

## OXFORD
UNIVERSITY PRESS

Great Clarendon Street, Oxford, OX2 6DP,
United Kingdom

Oxford University Press is a department of the University of Oxford.
It furthers the University's objective of excellence in research, scholarship,
and education by publishing worldwide. Oxford is a registered trade mark of
Oxford University Press in the UK and in certain other countries

© Oliver P. Richmond 2014

The moral rights of the author have been asserted

First Edition published in 2014
Impression: 2

All rights reserved. No part of this publication may be reproduced, stored in
a retrieval system, or transmitted, in any form or by any means, without the
prior permission in writing of Oxford University Press, or as expressly permitted
by law, by licence or under terms agreed with the appropriate reprographics
rights organization. Enquiries concerning reproduction outside the scope of the
above should be sent to the Rights Department, Oxford University Press, at the
address above

You must not circulate this work in any other form
and you must impose this same condition on any acquirer

Published in the United States of America by Oxford University Press
198 Madison Avenue, New York, NY 10016, United States of America

British Library Cataloguing in Publication Data
Data available

Library of Congress Control Number: 2014942179

ISBN 978-0-19-965600-4

Printed in Great Britain by
Ashford Colour Press Ltd, Gosport, Hampshire

Links to third party websites are provided by Oxford in good faith and
for information only. Oxford disclaims any responsibility for the materials
contained in any third party website referenced in this work.

# Contents

# Acknowledgements

Thanks to Mike Pugh, Alison Watson, Lucy and Carmel Richmond, and Jasmin Ramovic for their assistance, as well as several anonymous reviewers, and quite a few others for their input and encouragement. I would also like to thank Andrea Keegan and Emma Ma at OUP for their careful support.

# List of Illustrations

# Introduction: the multiple dimensions of peace

'Peace': freedom from war, disturbance, or dissension
(entered the English Language in the 12th century);
quiet, stillness, concord (13th century); peacemaker
(15th century)

*Oxford Concise Dictionary of Etymology*

## A sketch

The story of peace is as old as the story of humanity itself, and
certainly as old as war. It is a story of progress, often in very
difficult circumstances, as this volume will illustrate. Historically,
peace has often been taken, as with the *Oxford English
Dictionary*'s definition, to imply an absence of overt violence or
war between or sometimes within states. War is often thought to
be the natural state of humanity, peace of any sort being fragile
and fleeting. This book challenges this view. Peace in its various
forms has been by far humanity's more common experience—as
the archaeological, ethnographic, and historic records indicate.
Much of history has been relatively peaceful and orderly, while
frameworks for security, law, redistribution of resources, and
justice have constantly been advancing. Peace has been at the
centre of the human experience, and a sophisticated version of
peace has now become widely accepted.

Peace can be organized domestically within the state, internationally through global organizations and institutions, or transnationally through actors whose ambit covers all of these levels. Peace can be public or private. Peace has often been a hidden phenomenon, subservient to power and interests. Many analysts prefer to imagine that public power (of domestic politicians, the military, or international officials) is responsible for order rather than social, economic, political, or cultural harmony. Furthermore, in the political economy of war and violence policymakers and media distribute information around the world, often making violence appear to be a more significant and profitable media event than peace. This perspective tends to dominate the understandings of politicians, bureaucrats, and international policymakers whose role is one of problem solving and crisis management. Due to material and time constraints, such mitigations tend to be limited and pragmatic. The longer-term aspiration for a self-sustaining peace via a process aimed at a comprehensive outcome has rarely been attained, even with the combined assistance—in recent times—of international donors, the UN, World Bank, military forces, or international NGOs.

Peace practices and theories have made huge advances throughout history. However, the fact that the story of peace is so rarely told—despite its ubiquity—is beneficial for powerful elites who see violence as a political or economic tool. It does not help that peace is a rather ambiguous concept. Authoritarian governments and powerful states have, throughout history, had a tendency to impose their version of peace on their own citizens as well as those of other states, as with the Soviet Union's suppression of dissent amongst its own population and those of its satellite states, such as East Germany or Czechoslovakia. Peace and war may be closely connected, such as when military force is deployed to make peace, as with North Atlantic Treaty Organization (NATO) airstrikes in Bosnia-Herzegovina in 1995 and in Yugoslavia in 1999. The former ended the Serb siege of Sarajevo, which had continued for three years, leading to the Dayton Peace Accords in 1995, and then later stopped the war in Kosovo in 1999, in which Serbs attempted to suppress ethnic Kosovar Albanian opposition to their rule, leading to the establishment of a UN mission in Kosovo. On the other hand, both George Orwell (1903–50), in his novel *1984*, and the French social theorist Michel Foucault (1926–84) noted the dangers of the relationship between war and peace in their well-known aphorisms: 'peace is war', 'war is peace'.

A wide range of sources indicate that the emergence of peace is closely associated with a variety of political, social, economic, and cultural struggles against the horrors of war and oppression. Peace activism has normally been based on campaigns for individual and group rights and needs, for material and legal equality between groups, genders, races, and religions, disarmament, and to build international institutions. This has required the construction of local, and international associations, networks, and institutions, which coalesced around widely accepted agendas. Peace activism supported internationally organized civil society campaigns against slavery in the 18th century, and for basic human dignity and rights ever since. Various peace movements have struggled for independence and self-determination, or for voting rights and disarmament (most famously perhaps, the Campaign for Nuclear Disarmament). Ordinary people can, and have often, mobilized for peace in societal terms using peaceful methods of resistance (as with Indian non-violent opposition to British rule in the 1920s until Independence in 1947).

There is controversy over whether peace or war is humanity's 'natural condition'. The political left claims there is a constant struggle against oppression to achieve justice and peace, but that only a broad version of peace is acceptable. Conversely, the right claims that violence is endemic and inherent in human society and so a narrow version is the only pragmatic choice for the state. However, there is a wealth of evidence that supports a popular desire for a broad form of peace. It may also be that society is often more sensitized to peace issues than elites, states, institutions, politicians, policymakers, and bureaucrats. The latter tend to focus on a narrower set of interests driven by demands for security and profit whereas society requires an everyday peace to prosper and, lacking direct forms of power, experiences the vicissitudes of war and conflict most acutely.

This short book outlines the positive, though controversial, story of the evolution of peace in practice and theory (and mainly from the perspective of the global north). It should be noted that non-Western peace traditions, spanning the major historical civilizations, religions, and identities, have also provided important contributions. The West has been the loudest and most influential voice—for better or worse—in defining the politics and economics of peace since the Enlightenment at least. It has led the development of what is now known as the 'liberal peace', upon which the post-World War II and post-Cold War international architecture has been based. Since the early 2000s, a neoliberal peace has gradually taken over. Increasingly, more critical and/or non-Western voices are having their say on the debate about peace, however. The search continues for refinements of these models or for better, perhaps hybrid, alternatives in an increasingly post-colonial and post-liberal world.

# Chapter 1
# Defining peace

> As Peace, am I not praised by both men and gods as the very
> source and defender of all good things? What is there of
> prosperity, of security, or of happiness that cannot be
> ascribed to me? On the other hand, is not war the destroyer
> of all things and the very seed of evil?
>
> Desiderius Erasmus, *The Complaint of Peace*

Defining peace and its dimensions is a difficult task. There is no
single definition. A starting point is to think in terms of a narrow
version, which implies the ending of violence but not resolving its
underlying causes. The current situation in Cyprus where Greek
and Turkish Cypriot military forces, or Korea where North and
South Korean forces, confront each other daily across a
demilitarized line might be described as peace, according to this
framework. By contrast a broad version would produce a peace
agreement, peaceful state, and society according to a single
universal model. The European Union's emergence from the ruins
of World War II might be an example, where very similar states
have emerged. Finally, multiple versions of peace would imply the
coexistence, but simultaneous agreement to differ, of very
different social and political systems. Perhaps the peace
agreement between Egypt and Israel in 1978 is a good example of
this approach, in which very different states and their population,
with many remaining and deep disagreements and difference,

are reconciled, to a limited degree. Another example is offered by the form of peace that is emerging in Timor Leste since the Indonesian occupation ended in 1999. This partly follows the model offered by the modern state, in which democracy, law, human rights, and development provide a framework in which conflicts are managed by institutions, law, and increased prosperity. It is also combined with very different customs and systems of authority that exist at the community level, including customary forms of governance and processes of conflict resolution, including those historically used by elders, long-standing customary law, and well-known traditional reconciliation ceremonies called 'Tara bandu'. In 2013, the country's President recognized the important of these approaches, especially as they are closer to the population's culture than the modern state is, and the Timorese parliament is debating the possibility of incorporating these cultural resolution practices into the formal legal system.

Each of these versions of peace offers different levels of security and rights for society: a narrow version would be basic but relatively insecure, a broader version more complex but also more sustainable, and a multiple approach even more complex but stable. Underlying each type is a central question: does one make peace by subjugating one's enemies, assimilating them by converting them into something similar to the dominant group, or by accepting, and thus becoming reconciled to their difference?

According to Johan Galtung, one of the founders of modern peace studies, a 'negative peace' is the aim of narrow versions (which would be a good description of the failed peace treaty after World War I), a 'positive peace' the aim of broader versions (which may well explain the European Peace after World War II). A more recent concept, a 'hybrid peace', is the amalgam of multiple approaches (as may be emerging in places such as Timor Leste or Kosovo after the conflicts there in the late 1990s). A narrow understanding of peace indicates an absence of overt violence (such as warfare or low-intensity conflict) both between and within states. This may take the form of a ceasefire, a power-sharing agreement, or exist within an authoritarian political system. It indicates that one state, or group in society, dominates another through violence or more subtle means. This approach has the benefit of simplicity, but a negative peace will always be fragile because it is based on ever-shifting configurations of power in the international system or within the state. Hidden, so-called 'structural violence' embedded in social, economic, and political systems remains unaddressed. This might explain why, after various ceasefires in the 2000s, the peace process has collapsed in Colombia on several occasions, because the core issues of the dispute, in particular relating to land distribution, poverty, and socio-economic inequality, have not as yet been addressed. A peace agreement based on a narrow understanding of peace would probably not be satisfactory in anything other than the short term. Military force or an authoritarian government may maintain a basic security order—as in East Germany during the Cold War—but many deficits relating to human rights, democratic representation, and prosperity remain.

These remaining issues are markers of structural violence—meaning the indirect violence that is created by oppressive structures of government, of law, bureaucracy, trade, resource distribution, social class, or because of poverty or environmental problems. Sometimes structural violence can occur even in relatively peaceful societies.

A negative understanding of peace draws on an 'inherency' view of conflict. That is, violence is intrinsic to human nature, is part of our biology, and thus is endemic in society, history, and amongst states at the international level. Such an argument is often drawn from observations of how animals appear to behave, particularly primates (though the applicability of such evidence is much disputed). Negative peace may also refer to the tensions that global capitalism produces for societies disrupted by its 'creative destruction'. Little can be done about it other than to try to curb its worst excesses. It is easy to agree with such a position when taking a view of history that focuses only on its most visible and often violent moments, such as international or civil wars.

If conflict is endemic because it is rooted in human nature then little can be done about it other than using force to promote strategic interests. This represents a conservative and somewhat old-fashioned view of the politics of peace and war. Security in these terms means the preservation of a pre-existing hierarchy of states, their territorial sovereignty, and a balance of power between them—as in 19th century Europe and the 'Concert System' post-1815. This was the attitude toward war and conflict and their relationship with a negative peace (with honourable exceptions) from ancient times until at least the Enlightenment, perhaps even until the emergence of fascism in the early 20th century. Peace existed (somewhat conveniently for, and from, the perspective of kings, queens, emperors, and various dictators) mainly as a painful stalemate between rulers, or absolute victory, in between the frequent wars that took place across history. In this history, human beings are merely pawns of the powerful and their interests. Such views have slowly been supplanted by positive peace approaches since the Enlightenment.

A broader understanding of peace indicates both the lack of open violence between and within states, and the aim of creating the conditions for society to live without fear or poverty, within a broadly agreed political system. It implies the relative fulfilment of individuals in society, as well as stable political institutions, law, economics, states, and regions. It represents the proverbial 'good life' or the 'Perpetual Peace' to which famous philosophers from Aristotle (384–322 BC) to Immanuel Kant, a German liberal philosopher (1724–1804), have often alluded. Much of the post-Enlightenment political history, especially since the Treaty of Westphalia brought peace to a large part of Europe in 1648, reflects an attempt to develop a scientific conceptualization of peace in positive terms.

Thus, it may well be a myth that conflict is inherent in human nature. This negative peace story is propagated through the flawed observation of primate violence and Darwinian assumptions that human nature follows the same pattern. Such social-Darwinist arguments work in the interests of those who control resources and power—a conservative and elitist grouping. By contrast, even in the animal world, primates display impulses of social order and peacemaking. So it is possible to claim that in fact peacemaking has been the most common activity of humanity in history. As every society has experienced conflict on various levels, all societies have developed sophisticated methods for peacemaking—from social institutions to formal legal processes and public government institutions. Contrary to the inherency view, conflict and war are learned behaviours. Human action can prevent or mitigate conflict through institutions, compromise, agreement, redistribution of resources, and education. This view has shaped the attempt during the 20th century to build a positive peace, defined as long-term stability, sustainability, and social justice. From this understanding developed mediation, as used by US President Carter after the 1974 war in the Middle East between Egypt and Israel, peacekeeping as in Cyprus, Congo, and many other countries, conflict resolution and transformation now widely used at the civil society level, and peacebuilding as used from Cambodia to Bosnia-Herzegovina in the 1990s. Such strategies have often been based on security guarantees, such as by the USA or NATO.

A public or official narrative of history tends to be dominated by elites (kings, queens, emperors, politicians, the military, religious figures, the very rich, and, more often, men). However, there is also a private transcript of everyday history that offers a more nuanced understanding of human history and society. In this private transcript, a positive peace becomes visible as located in everyday life—perhaps akin to Aristotle's 'good life'. This social and 'natural' peacemaking tendency may be less visible than the ruptures caused by violence but nonetheless it represents the business of everyday life and contributions to the development of political and international institutions—from parliaments to the UN system.

From this perspective, contemporary developments in thinking about peace have moved far beyond a negative peace towards an investigation of what an emancipatory, everyday, empathetic form might look like in specific social contexts around the world (from Afghanistan to Liberia, for example) as well as in the architecture of the contemporary international system. This has engendered a shift from traditional notions of security where the onus was on the state to secure its territory and sovereignty, as Max Weber (1864–1920), one of the founders of sociology, argued. This view has also been replaced more recently by a version of security where human beings, rather than the state, are the main focus.

## A positive peace

A positive peace, along with concepts such as 'human security' (which in 1994 was defined by a UN Development Programme official as 'freedom from fear, freedom from want'), would be a higher priority than state security, and arguments that violence is learned rather than innate in society imply that conflict may be mutually and consensually resolved. Thus, a broad and inclusive form of peace may arise. Direct and structural violence can be removed. This peace is acceptable in everyday terms to ordinary people, not only to political and economic elites according to their interests. Such a situation transcends basic security concerns over power, territory, and material resources and offers a peace that is akin to the everyday lives that many people experience in developed liberal democracies, in which security, law, order, and prosperity are comparatively and relatively routine. Under such conditions social justice—human rights, democratic representation, relative material equality, and prosperity—the accountability of states and elites, as well as peace between states may be achieved.

Such a high-quality version of peace has rarely been achieved after war, unless in a longer-term perspective, as with most of the affected countries after World War II. This view rejects the argument that conflict is inherent in human nature and hence in states and institutions, but maintains instead that conflict can be resolved fully by people, states, and institutions. Human beings have the capacity to understand why conflict arises and to develop a range of innovative responses to it. These peace-oriented humans are not subjects of the powerful, but are politically engaged in local, everyday as well as transnational or international peace campaigns, institutions, and architectures. The significance of such an approach lies in its assumption that the nature and causes of conflict stem from many different dynamics. These may include social, economic, politic, military, and resource dynamics, such as identity, class, or ethnic differences, unfair, weak, and unrepresentative political institutions, or contests over resources such as land, oil, minerals, or labour.

Such multiple and entwined causes require multidimensional and sophisticated responses, if conflict is to be resolved. Because of this line of thought, the disciplines of international relations, political science, peace and conflict research, as well as law, sociology, anthropology, development, and economics, have all become essential to a more comprehensive understanding of the necessary conditions of peace in modern times.

The concept of a positive peace has been significant in policy terms because it reflects the growing demands of populations for their rights and needs to be met, and for essential public services to be provided in order to transcend the identity, religious, material, ideological, and territorial differences that have historically often sparked violence. It influences how conflict is understood and addressed by states and by various international or regional organizations: the UN, World Bank, and international donors or governments especially those of the OECD and G20, as well as the European Union. It provides essential 'navigation points for policy' whereby they are able to satisfy their electorates and citizens.

A further alternative to positive peace is that there exist multiple conceptions of peace across the range of cultures, states, and societies around the world. Most societies, however 'modern' or 'traditional', have their own version. These often engender different, or at least nuanced, notions of social harmony, economic prosperity, political institutions, and law, as well as respect for historical traditions and identity. Enabling coexistence between different entities practising different forms of peace would require mediation between them and cooperation at the social, state, and international level. This is most probably the next threshold for peace theory and practices to cross in their search for ever more advanced forms.

However peace is defined, it has always attracted innovative or radical thought, action (often heroic in nature), and has led to improved institutions and practices. Although there have been sophisticated intellectual debates about peace throughout history, peace has also often been defined by power rather than justice.

The history of peace in Western and often 'Eurocentric' thought spans the thought of the ancient Greek philosopher Plato to the emergence of NATO after World War II, the recent history of European integration, and its attempts to develop regional cooperation between former enemies. Over the years of its existence, the UN (often through the General Assembly or its many agencies) has compiled and released documents, reports, and resolutions resting on a wide global consensus. These have pointed to strategies designed to deal with the adverse connection between power and peace: from its programmes for 'cultures of peace', rights to peace, on the need for 'new economic orders', economic, social and cultural rights, to independence, self-determination, development, and peacebuilding. These all called for equality in identity and gender terms, self-determination, participation, cooperation, social justice, and development. They have endorsed a right to culture, society, and work, and to choose one's own identity. They have called for an international states-system framed in the interests of positive, rather than negative, peace, interests, or power. Representatives of much of the planet's population signed these documents, yet such global political and scientific consensus has been easily forgotten. Thus, the evolution of peace has been slow, and rather than a single, positive, universal peace emerging, this process appears to be leading to an interlocking system of multiple 'peaces'. In its most simple terms this might be seen in the wide varieties of states that currently coexist: from Western liberal democracies, to China's authoritarian capitalism, the Gulf States, or the many developing democracies containing populations with widely different configurations of identity and religion, including Brazil, South Africa, and the likes of Sri Lanka, Cambodia, or Colombia.

In the contemporary era, more active terms such as 'peacebuilding', 'conflict resolution', and 'statebuilding' are often used interchangeably, especially by scholars and policymakers, with the word 'peace'. The modern concept of peace has broadened from the mere absence of violence. Within the UN system policymakers generally agree that they should try to address the root causes of conflict. Peace has also been associated with active resistance to subtle forms of domination, as well as to the inequalities that global capitalism often produces (especially because extractive multinational corporations (MNCs) are often the first businesses to arrive in post-conflict countries after a peace agreement, to exploit the country's natural resources).

There are untold disruptions present but unrecognized in all of our lives because of past wars. Yet, the story of peace is more pervasive in terms of the measure of time that humanity has experienced it. Peacetime involves not just the absence of violence but also the mundanities of everyday life. To an eye trained to look for military conflict these aspects of peace may be inconsequential. Peace's broader aspects, which St Augustine, the Latin theologian of the 4th–5th centuries AD, called the 'tranquillity of order', are often taken for granted. Peace is the most long-term aspect of human experience, even if it may appear or feel banal, everyday, and ordinary.

## Theoretical approaches to peace

Several important lines of thought converge in theoretical approaches to peace: one focused on the constitution of the state, another on the role of international organizations, another on the underlying philosophy of peace, and another on social peace movements emerging from society. Peace also has had religious connotations, arising from the way different religions treat violence and promote tolerance throughout history. Such views span concepts such as 'just war', self-defence, non-violence, and pacifism, drawing on Christian, Buddhist, and Hindu philosophy.

Some general theories, dynamics, and themes prominent in the historical discussion of peace reappear in theory. The best-known approach in political theory is called *political realism*. Contributors include authors such as Sun Tzu (an ancient Chinese military strategist and philosopher who was the author of *The Art of War* in the 6th century BC), Thucydides (an ancient Greek historian from the 5th century BC, who because of his experiences in the Peloponnesian War between Sparta and Athens claimed that power rather than morality was important in war), and Augustine (a Latin philosopher and theologian during the late Roman Empire in the 5th century AD). Realism mainly focuses on the military (and later on economic) power of states.

Machiavelli, an Italian historian, politician, diplomat, and philosopher based in Florence during the Renaissance, worried that peace might lead to disorder, requiring a military response (in his famous book *The Prince*, published around 1532):

> A wise prince ought to observe some such rules, and never in peaceful times stand idle, but increase his resources with industry in such a way that they may be available to him in adversity, so that if fortune changes it may find him prepared to resist her blows. (Chapter XIV)

Nevertheless, the common view that the ancient period was defined by an acceptance of the inevitability of war is perhaps mistaken. Even Machiavelli, more often associated with power and interests, thought that elections were necessary and peace should be fair and voluntary.

Later, in Enlightenment philosophy, Thomas Hobbes's *Leviathan* (1651) set out social contract theory, including the need for political representation, individual rights, and notions of civil society. Drawing on his experience of the English civil war, Hobbes argued for a social contract between the population and an absolute sovereign (called a Leviathan after a biblical monster). He thought that a 'war of all against all' required a Leviathan in the form of a strong central government.

Peace was understood in a relatively narrow way in realist thought, in which it was defined by merely the absence of open violence. However, structural violence might be present. Key modern scholars and policy figures in this tradition like Henry Kissinger (born in 1923, a scholar and Secretary of State for Presidents Richard Nixon and Gerald Ford), influenced by experiences in World War II and during the Cold War, often see peace mainly as a balance of power between states.

Another important approach draws on ancient critiques of militarism, following those of Confucius (a 6th century BC Chinese philosopher), that war would not give rise to peace. Government should focus on the well-being of the people, not on making war. Given the legitimacy and attractiveness of peace, it has often been central to any civilization's narrative about its place in the world. In the case of China, Confucius himself said that 'pacific harmony' bound society together. He offered his famous aphorism that peace extended from the heart to the family, then to society, and to the world. Daoism also connected inner, social, and collective harmony, which also incidentally required a norm of non-interference. Even during the Warring States period of Chinese history, famous voices decried war (and the realist propositions of Sun Tzu) in favour of the merits of peace. Confucius' focus on 'civil virtues' was the most famous of these: among other wise statements, he argued in his book *Analects*, '… [r]ecompense injury with justice, and recompense kindness with kindness'. His work has more recently been reclaimed as an emblem of modern China's 'peaceful development'.

From classical Greece to ancient China, war was a disruption of a 'natural' and peaceful order, rather than the other way around. Respect, civil virtue, neighbourliness, cooperation, morality, trade, good governance, kinship, and treaties are motifs of early representations of peace. Another characteristic of early thinking on peace was the relationship with government and citizens, from Plato onwards. Peace is in the interests of a 'philosopher-king' who exercises his judgement for the good of all, however difficult this may be, according to Plato's *Republic*. In addition, in ancient Greek philosophy around the 3rd century BC, the Epicureans crystallized a growing concern with everyday conditions for ordinary people, and the Stoics rejected the passions of greed, anger, or lust, calling for self-discipline and solidarity. Even at this early stage, individuals were mobilizing for peace, realizing that their local and social environment was crucial, that peace required different types of approaches, and that it had an international dimension.

These approaches were associated with issues of abundance and dignity (as with the Greek goddess Eirene, who was the personification of peace, often depicted in art as a beautiful young daughter of Zeus carrying a cornucopia). They also suggested a rejection of war through various strategies, as exemplified in Aristophanes' comic play *Lysistrata*. Eventually there emerged a historical build-up of diplomatic peace treaties in ancient Greece reflecting such understandings, which became ever more refined and widespread, aiming at creating a 'common peace'.

Another contribution to this process drew on the thinking of the Christian philosopher Augustine, who himself reflected a longer historical tradition. This is known as 'just war'. In his book *Summa Theologica*, Augustine wrote:

> A just war is wont to be described as one that avenges wrongs, when a nation or state has to be punished, for refusing to make amends for the wrongs inflicted by its subjects, or to restore what it has seized unjustly.

Thomas Aquinas (AD 1225–74) later developed this in some detail. War was deemed just if it was in self-defence, punished aggression (but was not for revenge), was undertaken by the authorities, or was a last resort. It should ultimately make peace. This framework has persisted in international relations until this day, reinvented as humanitarian intervention and regime change war by the 1990s in Bosnia-Herzegovina and the 2000s in Iraq, respectively. Just war aided peace, and peace was itself a natural and necessary outcome of war according to this influential view. Just war thinking influences political discussions today, even if indirectly, as during the invasion of Iraq in 2003.

Theories such as idealism and liberalism are closely related to these debates, and are often associated with the theories of Immanuel Kant and his plan for 'Perpetual Peace'.

The concept of peace has also been enriched by Marxist thinking about oppression, power and class struggle, exploitation, and revolutionary change, driven, partly at least, by grassroots actors. This has given rise to understandings of peace that include social justice and emancipation, with important implications for the poor, women, and children. (The idea of violent revolutionary change, associated with some variants of Marxism, presents a conundrum for peace.) Gramscian understandings of the potential of mobilization of grassroots actors for their rights have also been important.

It is important to note a division in the understanding of peace amongst the various schools of peace studies around the world. Some see it as a contribution to maintaining the dominant liberal and capitalist world order, which for many outside of the global north is a negative peace. More critical approaches see peace as connected to social justice and emancipation, meaning human rights, equality, solidarity, and sustainability, required for a positive peace. Some claim that Eurocentric norms and institutions dominate global governance often at the expense of the general population. Most schools argue that they are aiming at a positive peace, of course. Most of these arguments are critical of realist approaches to peace. There is also a post-modern perspective indicating the necessity of social justice, participatory forms of democracy, human rights, equality, and autonomy. Such views also generally posit that no one perspective has a monopoly on defining peace. Multiple forms must therefore coexist.

A range of critical and post-colonial theorists foresaw the increasing demands made of the concept of peace. Some highlighted the rights and needs of humanity, problems arising from global capitalism and neoliberalism, the inherent biases of liberalism, and the capacity for peoples to mobilize for social justice, equality, and freedom. Among many these included: Paulo Freire (a Brazilian philosopher (1921–97), who wrote *Pedagogy of the Oppressed*); Frantz Fanon (a French-Algerian writer (1925–61) whose works inspired anti-colonial liberation movements); Homi Bhabha (a post-colonial theorist (1949–) who showed how hybrid political frameworks arise from the ways in which colonized peoples resist the power of the colonizer); and Amartya Sen (an Indian economist (1933–) who won the 1998 Nobel Memorial Prize in Economics and helped to create the United Nations Human Development Index, which compares and ranks each country's state of development). These more critical views of peace seek to uncover power and its workings and establish a fairer form of domestic and international politics, more likely to lead to a positive, or even hybrid, form of peace.

One theory has dominated the modern debate on peace so far, however. The liberal peace theory suggests that democracy ensures that domestic politics within states are peaceful. Together with free trade it also ensures that states do not then go to war with each other, following the sole 'law' of international relations that democratic states do not fight each other (but instead cooperate and trade) so leading to a relatively peaceful, though perhaps imperfect, regional and international order. This argument has often been used as an explanation for the stability of Europe after World War II, in contrast to its earlier history.

At the international level, the liberal peace has been supported by international institutions, which during the 20th century facilitated cooperation between states over problems such as disarmament and arms control and supported free trade and common norms, rules, and laws. Since the end of the Cold War in 1990, the West has reiterated the related argument that peace requires democratic and human rights observing states, free trade, a cosmopolitan recognition of diverse identities, and coexistence at the community level. There has been a political and scholarly consensus around these factors, especially in the global north. In the global south, a related consensus has been growing, despite the fact that it has often not benefited equally from the global economic conditions.

Such thinking has continued to evolve and a further contribution has been offered by contemporary liberal thinkers (including the American scholars John Rawls, Michael Walzer, and Michael Doyle) and policymakers. They have also connected Kant's liberal peace with the capacity to wage 'just war' (meaning wars, often called 'humanitarian intervention' or 'regime change', may be legitimate if they support the non-proliferation of weapons and protect human rights, democracy, and a rule of law).

The liberal peace aimed to balance the interests of states and their societies, to maintain some elite level interests, but also to a large degree to assuage the concerns of society, all within an international architecture of peace determined by international organizations and law. It represents a balance between freedom, social justice, and mutual regulation, designed to prevent war and domestic conflict. Failing to address issues in one or several of these essential elements may undermine a positive form of peace. Though flawed it probably represents one of the most sophisticated forms in history.

The liberal peace framework can be broken down into a number of intellectual and practical traditions:

1.  the **victor's peace** in which a negative peace is imposed by a victor in war;
2.  the **constitutional peace** in which democracy and free trade are taken to be fundamental qualities of any peaceful state's constitution (contributing to a positive peace);
3.  the **institutional peace**, in which international institutions, such as the UN, international financial institutions (e.g. the Bretton Woods institutions), state donors, act to maintain peace and order according to a mutually agreed framework of international law (contributing to a positive peace);
4.  the **civil peace** tradition in which civil society organizations, NGOs, and domestic and transnational social movements seek to uncover and rectify historical injustice or processes that engender the risk of war (contributing to a positive peace).

The current fragility of the post-Cold War order has again reopened the question of what is peace? Should it follow the Western model of liberal peace or are there other alternatives? In the 21st century, a neoliberal peace appears to have become dominant in international policy, where the focus is more on deregulation and free-market reforms than human rights and democracy. However, there is widespread concern that it does not meet the standards required for a positive form of peace.

# Chapter 2
# Peace in history

> Peace shines on human affairs like the vernal sun. The fields
> are cultivated, the gardens bloom, the cattle are fed upon a
> thousand hills, new buildings arise, riches flow, pleasures
> smile, humanity and charity increase, arts and manufactures
> feel the genial warmth of encouragement, and the gains of
> the poor are more plentiful....
>
> Desiderius Erasmus, *The Complaint of Peace*, 1521

## Introduction: diverse historical sources

Wars, conflicts, and uprisings during the last two decades, in
Afghanistan, Iraq, the Middle East, and North Africa, among
others, illustrate the significance of violence for contemporary
international relations. However, contrary to what some believe,
peace is neither a 'modern invention' nor is it particularly scarce.
There is a vast corpus of sources that make this clear: historical,
social, religious, political and economic, artistic and cultural, as
well as policies, theories, and philosophies. Many, if not all,
illustrate the integral nature of peace in the fabric of everyday life,
society, the state, and international relations throughout history.
They also often indicate an aspiration for a positive or hybrid form
in replacement for extant negative forms of peace.

Peace has been invoked in many different ways across history. The Cyrus Cylinder (6th century BC) is thought to be an early Persian declaration of human rights. Peace is also represented in early political philosophy such as in the thought of Confucius (551 BC–479 BC). In classical literature such as Aristophanes' *Lysistrata* (*c*.411 BC), Lysistrata persuades the women of Greece to withhold sexual privileges from their partners to force the men to negotiate peace. Peace underlies legal documents such as England's foundational Magna Carta (1215), which protected men and property before the law. There has always been an 'art' of peace, such as in Renaissance painter Ambrogio Lorenzetti's *Allegory of Good and Bad Government* (1338–9) (see Figure 1). There is a literary approach, as in Desiderius Erasmus' Enlightenment play *The Complaint of Peace*, in which a personified Peace complains of being ignored and treated unjustly.

A widely held historical belief is that humanity cannot fulfil its potential without peace. There exists a 'will to peace' just as there is also a Nietzschean 'will to power'. Erasmus put this eloquently in the epigraph for this chapter. While there will always be conflict and self-interest, society has always mobilized for peace in response.

## Key dimensions of peace in history

In ancient Mesopotamia, it was recognized that peace protects life, law, and customs, whereas war is aggressive and risks retaliation, as the Mosaic of Ur (*c*.2650 BC) portrays. Similarly, in the heroic Mesopotamian poem *Gilgamesh*, the hero's downfall is caused by his failure to preserve peace. The implication is clear. As in many of the world's religions, a historical propensity towards non-violence (though sometimes after a victory in war), enlightenment, honesty, and integrity is generally presented as crucial to a peace that begins with the community and everyday life and then extends to the world.

Peace

1. Two sections from Lorenzetti's *Allegory of Good and Bad Government* (1338–9) depicts the benefits of good government on a city

From a popular perspective either a 'victor's peace' (in negative form) or an 'ideal form' underpins the dominant understanding of peace. In Plato's (428/427 BC–348/347 BC) *Republic*, Socrates repeated the view that truth represents an ideal form associated with 'goodness'. Individuals, communities, leaders, states, or empires often subscribe to such an ideal form of peace.

Thus, peace treaties have influenced the story of human history as much as wars or the succession of kings, queens, emperors, dictators, or elected leaders. They span examples such as the Kadesh Treaty (around 1274 BC) (see Figure 2) between the Hittite and Egyptian Empires to the much more recent Comprehensive Peace Agreement signed between the two Sudanese sides in 2005. The peace treaty was used commonly to end wars and stabilize regions: famous examples include the Pax Nicephori of AD 803 between the Roman Emperor Charlemagne and the Byzantine

2. **The Kadesh Treaty, from around 1274 BC, was one of the first ever recorded peace treaties between the Egyptian and Hittite Empires**

Empire; the Treaty of Venice of 1177 between the Catholic Pope, the north Italian city-states of the Lombard League, and Frederick I, the Holy Roman Emperor; or the Treaty of Perpetual Peace between England and Scotland in 1502 (see Figure 3). Perhaps most significant was the Treaty of Westphalia in 1648 bringing to an end a cycle of European wars. Other examples include the Paris Peace Treaty giving independence to the USA from Britain in 1783; the more famous Paris Peace Treaty at Versailles in 1919 after World War I; and the UN Charter in 1945, which was essentially a peace treaty for the modern world. Other more recent examples include the Camp David Agreement between Egypt and Israel in 1978 bringing to an end a cycle of wars between them; the Oslo Accords between Israel and the Palestinians in 1993; and the Dayton Agreement for Bosnia-Herzegovina in 1995, which through US pressure brought to an end the conflict between Serbs, Bosniacs, and Croats after three years of war.

Understandings of religious tolerance are also commonly connected with peace, represented for example in Christianity by non-violence and pacifism. Similarly, there are the Buddhist and Hindi notions of *shanti* and *ahimsa*, which represent first an inner peace and then a wider peace. Islam and Sufi offer an understanding of peace as an internal quest within everyone, which when achieved may lead to an 'outer peace'. Hinduism, Buddhism, Christianity, Judaism, and Islam all make such claims in various different ways. Judaism associates peace with a sectarian identity within a universal peace. Christianity famously blessed its peacemakers in following suit. Islam demanded that any attempt at peacemaking should always be reciprocal and that individuals should be at peace before a wider peace can emerge. Most religions also warn of 'false peacemakers'. By the 10th century onward, a movement organized by the Catholic Church called the 'Peace of God' lobbied feudal elites and warlords to commit to peace rather than war. By the 11th century, a number of peace councils had been held in France, which the Pope supported, even though the Crusades were in full swing. In the

3. The Treaty of Perpetual Peace signed by James IV of Scotland and Henry VII of England ended, for a time at least, 200 years of sporadic warfare between Scotland and England

last years of the 12th century, Richard the Lionheart commissioned his knights to keep order across his kingdom, calling them 'Justices of the Peace'. In the 13th century, the famous 'Prayer for Peace' appeared (attributed to Francis of Assisi): 'Lord, make me an instrument of Thy peace; where there is hatred, let me sow love...' Many religious orders began to emphasize peace.

Another early dimension of peace arose from pacts and leagues formed both to stabilize political relations and enable trade, such the Hanseatic League of the 12th century. This was a commercial and defensive confederation of merchant guilds that controlled trade from the Baltic to the North Sea during the 13th–17th centuries. Others followed as European imperialism and colonialism gathered pace during the 16th and ensuing centuries, often between colonizers and local leaders, or between colonial powers that were seeking to demarcate their area of influence. Peace in these terms followed, and was secondary to, power and trade.

Perhaps one of the most famous early legal instruments of peace within a state was the English Magna Carta. This bound even the king to the law (a radical idea in the 13th century), and introduced some basic aspects of human rights, including the principle of *Habeas Corpus* (meaning a citizen cannot be imprisoned without a fair trial) (see Figure 4).

Domestic peace was not the only preoccupation of government and law. Dante Alighieri, an early Florentine humanist, published an important book called *On World Government* in 1309, which outlined how a world government and related justice system may resolve local conflicts, allowing each nation to develop its specific capacities in peacetime: '...[e]very kingdom divided against itself shall be laid waste...' To prevent this '...there must therefore be one person who directs and rules mankind, and he is properly called "Monarch" or "Emperor". And thus it is apparent that the well-being of the world requires that there be a monarchy or empire' (Book 1). The idea of a world government, bound by law,

Peace

4. In 1215 the Magna Carta limited the powers of the King of England and protected his subjects' rights, forming the basis for the rule of law

became a long-standing motif of many peace movements. The state, government, and a concept of the 'international' now began to emerge as recognized components of a broader approach to peace.

Francisco de Vitoria (1483–1546), a Spanish Renaissance philosopher and jurist, offered the idea of the formation of a 'republic of the whole world'. He stated that the safety of diplomats should be assured, peace talks should be held to pre-empt conflict, and there should be a general acceptance of just terms. He also saw that it might be necessary to allow military intervention to prevent oppression. These terms should be the right of neutrality, safe passage, restraint in the conduct of warfare (especially with regard to civilians).

By the 1500s, Erasmus had emerged as a major advocate of peace. The peace he imagined was not based on an order preserved by war, religion, or national identity. Erasmus was part of an emerging humanist tradition focused on how the internal structure of a state influenced its behaviour and how its Christian rulers should behave. This approach also called for binding arbitration processes between states over their conflicts.

In Erasmus' play *Complaint of Peace* (1517), a personified Peace said:

> ...am I not praised by both men and gods as the very source and defender of all good things? What is there of prosperity, of security, or of happiness that cannot be ascribed to me? On the other hand, is not war the destroyer of all things and the very seed of evil?

This was published one year after Thomas More (1478–1535), another famous English Renaissance philosopher and humanist, published *Utopia* (1516), which explored the possibly of achieving a political and social utopia. Erasmus' work also prepared the ground for Hugo Grotius (1583–1645), a Dutch jurist and philosopher, to develop international law.

## Towards a modern view

International law has become an essential (though often maligned) part of the modern international system and its approach to peace. Such humanist explorations for peace appeared to have reached a summit with the 'Treaty of Universal Peace' in 1520, negotiated by Cardinal Wolsey between England and France, which offered hope that a wider European peace could for once be achieved. Erasmus later went on to advise the Prince, contra Machiavelli, to avoid war, regard the welfare of his people as he would his family, have his advisers approved by his people, and offer justice, laws, and education. As Erasmus noted in the *Complaint of Peace*, this era was to end violently. Even so, he noted that '... [h]ardly any peace is so bad that it is not preferable to the most just war'.

Underlying such thinking was a growing sense of how domestic and international order should be maintained. As representative political institutions in European states began to emerge, partly in response to such pressures, slowly replacing feudalism, parliaments began to emerge or re-form across Europe to assuage citizens who had begun to sense their capacity to lobby for, make, and preserve peace and social justice. Avoiding war, violence, conscription, and related tax burdens, as well as other indirect consequences of war, was becoming a political aim of increasingly demanding populations.

Peace has often formally been 'made' by enlightened political and social leaders. Understandably, peace has often been thought of as emerging from diplomatic, elite, and high-level negotiations, based on a trading of interests according to the 'red lines' delineated by state interests and their relative power. A painting of the Somerset House Conference in London from 1604 commemorates this approach. The conference brought to an end a twenty-year war between England and Spain.

Developments in peace thinking and practice were taking place further afield. In Japan, a neo-Confucian scholar and shogun, Tokugawa Ieyasu, laid the basis for the Tokugawa Peace, which lasted from 1603 to 1868. This period saw significant economic growth as well as cultural development, but Japan was also isolationalist and had a strict social order. European settlers and explorers in the Americas also encountered indigenous communities that followed historical non-violent codes of behaviour.

The flowering of peace thinking during the Enlightenment was intended to put an end to the lengthy and vicious cycle of elite-led or religious European wars. Perhaps the most famous of the European peace treaties of this era was the Treaty of Westphalia. This was actually a series of peace treaties signed in 1648 in Osnabrück and Münster, which ended several connected wars (see Figure 5). These included the Thirty Years War (1618–48) of the Holy Roman Empire, and the Eighty Years War (1568–1648) between Spain and the Dutch Republic. The Treaty created a political order of sovereign states in Europe with the right of territorial integrity. This meant the state would not be subject to invasion or intervention by other powers, a principle that still holds today (see UN Charter, Article 2/7). It was a precursor to future peace treaties and the development of international law, and the principle of self-determination.

The Enlightenment was partly the stimulus for an emerging idea that government, the state, and a system of international organizations should prioritize a general peace, rather than the vicarious interests of a few powerful actors. Important contributions were made by Hugo Grotius, and Emeric Cruce (1590–1648), who published a book in 1623 subtitled 'Establishing a General Peace and Freedom of Trade', which castigated bigotry, glory, and profit-seeking through war. William Penn (1644–1718), a philosopher, and founder of the Province of Pennsylvania, added his support for democracy and religious freedom. He began to

5. The Treaty of Westphalia was signed between May and October 1648 in Osnabrück and Munster, ending the Thirty Years War and the Eighty Years War

develop 'internationalist' thinking, whereby international cooperation was deemed crucial for peace to emerge.

John Locke, an English philosopher regarded as one of the most influential of Enlightenment thinkers (1632–1704), offered the liberal idea that individualism, religious tolerance, and equality as well as consensual government were crucial for peace. Most important were law and civil society in his view:

> And that all men may be restrained from invading others rights, and from doing hurt to one another, and the law of nature be observed, which willeth the peace and preservation of all mankind, the execution of the law of nature is, in that state, put into every man's hands, whereby everyone has a right to punish the transgressors of that law to such a degree, as may hinder its violation... (*The Second Treatise of Civil Government*, 1690)

34

William Penn's essay 'Towards the Present and Future Peace of Europe' (1693) contributed to a discussion about how to organize a sustainable European peace through a parliament for Europe. Rousseau (1712–78), a Genevan political philosopher who influenced the French Revolution, and Kant turned their attention to the refinement of a particular genre of European peace plan. In addition, Rousseau introduced the element of a contract between rulers and the people designed to balance the stability of the state with security as well as personal liberty, arguing: 'I prefer liberty with danger than peace with slavery.'

Kant's essay *Perpetual Peace* is the most famous contribution to peace thinking of all. He claimed that:

> The universal and lasting establishment of peace constitutes not merely a part, but the whole final purpose and end of the science of right as viewed within the limits of reason.

Kant's point-by-point articulation of a peaceful world order was as follows:

(1) No conclusion of Peace shall be held to be valid as such, when it has been made with the secret reservation of the material for a future War.

(2) No State having an existence by itself—whether it be small or large—shall be acquirable by another State through inheritance, exchange, purchase or donation.

(3) Standing Armies shall be entirely abolished in the course of time.

(4) No National Debts shall be contracted in connection with the external affairs of the State.

(5) No State shall intermeddle by force with the Constitution or Government of another State.

(6) No State at war with another shall adopt such modes of hostility as would necessarily render mutual confidence impossible in a future Peace...

He added to this the requirements that:

> The Civil Constitution in every State shall be Republican [meaning democratic].
> The Right of Nations shall be founded on a Federation of Free States.
> The Rights of men as Citizens of the world in a cosmo-political system, shall be restricted to conditions of universal Hospitality.

In other words, he called for the creation of an international organization to promote world peace, and for states to adopt democracy and human rights. These 'articles' have become the basis for the contemporary understanding of the democratic or liberal peace, which dominates international policy today. Such thinking has been crucial to the peace movements of the 20th century. It foreshadowed the establishment of international organization after World War II and a range of institutions, from the UN system to the EU and the African Union, as well as the contemporary mechanisms of peacemaking, peacebuilding, statebuilding, and humanitarian intervention.

## The importance of social advocacy

The discussion of peace had by then ceased to be dominated by kings, philosophers, religious figures, or political theorists. By the 19th century, with the birth of an array of social movements, activists, and lobbyists for peace, involving ordinary people who were determined to wrest the power of making war away from elites, it became clear that peace lay in their hands too.

Historically, a mixture of social movements have contributed to pressure for a significant change in politics and social structures, often in response to long-standing political, social, and economic inequalities across and between societies. They followed on from the success of the civil society movements against slavery in the 19th century and began to organize and mobilize across a range of other issue areas. For example in Britain, the Chartists, an amalgam of working-class organizations who desired political reform in Britain between 1838 and 1848, published their agenda for universal suffrage (for men at least), regular elections, and a professional political cohort (as opposed to a landed aristocracy). There was a socialist tinge to such developments along the path to what is now called 'social justice', whereby society and individuals pressed for equality rather than hierarchy, and for the 'proletariat' to resist exploitation and create a classless society.

Karl Marx's (1818–83) work was instrumental in the development of the socialist movement. It outlined the problems of capitalism from the perspective of the 'working classes'. In his book with another revolutionary socialist, Friedrich Engels, *The Communist Manifesto* (published in 1848), Marx criticized the structural oppression that capitalism and the old feudal system represented, supporting the provision of better conditions and rights for workers. He was, however, ambivalent about whether peaceful or revolutionary means were necessary. Such sentiments also reflected a broader social dissatisfaction with the hierarchical organization of power and class in the West.

A major international peace conference in Britain in 1843 saw support for free trade, pacifism, and peaceful means of conflict resolution begin to coalesce. Another conference was held in Paris the following year. Richard Cobden, one of the great English liberal thinkers of the day (1804–65), and Victor Hugo, the French poet and novelist (1802–85), were in attendance, illustrating the breadth of the appeal of such ambitions. At this meeting, the pace and pressures of development, the shrinking of the world due to better transport, the need for mediation, the habit of raising loans for wars were all discussed. There was disagreement, however, over the mutually exclusive agendas of disarmament, pacifism, the maintenance of security, and self-determination, which divided participants and continued to do so sporadically throughout the century. Peace was by now becoming openly politicized.

Organizations like the Fabian Society, founded in England in 1884, worked at improving social and working conditions and tempered any revolutionary intent with a Christian ethos. Even so, it was the implications of such thinking about social justice, spanning human rights and representation to a fairer distribution of power and resources across society, that produced one of the most powerful reformist dynamics of the 19th and 20th centuries.

Pacifism is often equated with peace movements (though not all are pacifist because some argue that there are occasions—such as for self-defence, to resist oppression, genocide, or imperialism—where violence may be justified). In general pacifists oppose war and violence of all sorts. Pacifism has been a feature of human history and all of the different world religions. Tolstoy's and Thoreau's writings on the need for pacifism and on civil disobedience become especially significant during this period. Leo Tolstoy (1828–1910) was the Russian author of *War and Peace*, and a noted moral thinker and social reformer, often described as a 'Christian anarchist' and pacifist. Tolstoy became famous for opposing militarism through civil disobedience and non-violent resistance. Henry David Thoreau (1817–62), an American philosopher, wrote an essay, 'Civil Disobedience', in which he called upon individuals to resist unjust states:

> If a thousand men were not to pay their tax bills this year, that would not be a violent and bloody measure, as it would be to pay them, and enable the State to commit violence and shed innocent blood. This is, in fact, the definition of a peaceable revolution, if any such is possible.

Increasingly, non-violent resistance aimed to overcome inequality and injustice and was adopted by large social interest groups. Such ideas on non-violent resistance were to have a profound impact, for example, on Mahatma Gandhi (1869–1948) during the Indian independence struggle from the British Empire in the first half of the 20th century, and also on Martin Luther King, Jr (1929–68), during his civil rights struggle in the USA.

Another aspect of peace thinking emerged from the work of one of the key early thinkers in the anarchist tradition, Pierre-Joseph Proudhon. He claimed in his study *War and Peace* (1861) that nation-states and the principle of private property would undermine peace. He thought that anarchism should be non-violent and systems of mutualism (whereby labour would receive a fair recompense rather than make profit for capitalists) should take over the formal processes of the state.

Similar themes were also on the agenda of the First and Second Internationals (1864–76 and 1889–1916) towards the end of the 19th century, which brought together a range of socialist and labour parties from around twenty different countries, to promote the rights of workers. Working men's associations, trade unions, socialists, and communists around the world, but most notably in Britain, tried (often unsuccessfully) to develop a united front on matters such as working rights and hours, gender equality, and a limited anti-war stance. Peace was beginning to be connected with the development of capitalism and its modes of production.

By the end of the 19th century, the emerging peace movements had involved or gained the attention of millions of people. They increasingly refused to be passive actors in elite-led wars and began to develop a range of political, philosophical, economic, and social arguments against war and for a better peace. Various 'friends of peace' movements in the West laid the basis for an organized peace movement to emerge there. In Britain and the USA, they united a range of thinkers, religious movements, labourers, scientists, writers, economists, social reformers, and activists. Their aim was to prevent rulers from seeing only benefit in war, but also to realize the potential of peace as well as popular demand for it. The Quakers, for example, equated pacifism and peace with religious positions connected to a broader struggle for justice and welfare (and today they quietly support civil society and formal peace processes throughout the world).

Furthermore, the increasingly industrial-scale conflicts of the 19th century, from the Crimean War to various Franco-Prussian wars from the 1850s to the 1870s, led to the emergence of another important strand of peace architecture. This lay in the beginnings of humanitarian law and of humanitarian relief organizations, notably the Red Cross. In 1859 Henri Dunant, a Swiss businessman, was an incidental witness of war. Horrified by his experience of the Battle of Solferini, he inspired the establishment of the International Red Cross in Geneva in 1863. The subsequent first Geneva Convention called for the humane treatment of all involved in war, including prisoners and humanitarian workers. It required that the Red Cross, a neutral international humanitarian relief agency, should have free access to war zones and its neutrality be respected by warring governments. Dunant was to be a joint recipient of the first Nobel Peace Prize in 1901.

The 19th century peace movement culminated in a number of congresses, movements, meetings, and conferences, including the 1899 conference at The Hague. This movement was becoming known as 'liberal internationalism', which developed the goal of formalizing the peace movement at the international level. One strand of this development sought to refine international law, another focused on creating an international federation of states, whilst another looked towards a world government, as the ultimate arbiter of peace. The 1899 conference introduced the idea of international arbitration as a means of dispute settlement (in which conflict parties agree to submit their disputes to binding resolution by a third party). This was supposed to be obligatory upon all of its state signatories, twenty-six of whom were present. No progress was made on the issue of disarmament. Further conferences were held in the early part of the 20th century, which also included women's peace movements, but the outbreak of World War I put such developments in abeyance until the League of Nations was formed by the victorious allies soon after.

The arts have also played their role in the development of the concept of peace, and its popularization. For example, Lorenzetti's 1340 frescos of *Peace and War* in Siena depicted the radically different impacts of peace and war on the city. Sometimes, peace is offered in subtle and unlikely forms, such as Rubens's famous painting *Minerva protects Pax from Mars* (1629–30), which was an illustration of the painter's role as unofficial envoy between England and Spain. During the 20th century peace continued to motivate or be reflected in numerous examples of modern art and culture, such as Picasso's *Guernica* (1937), which exposed modern industrial warfare against civilians, and in literature and war poetry, such as that of Wilfred Owen, British poet and a soldier in World War I (including *Dulce et Decorum Est* and *Anthem for Doomed Youth*, 1919).

Historically, a period of violence in any society has always spurred the development of peacemaking strategies to combat it, both from within society and by external actors. Many so-called 'peaceful societies' around the world, often of a small, tribal nature, have developed internal processes of conflict mediation, avoidance, and self-restraint. In modern times, some states have adopted 'peace constitutions', whereby they have little or no military capacity. Brazil now defines itself as 'pacific by tradition and conviction' according to its own Ministry of Defence (2005), as do many other states.

Peace has stimulated liberal political declarations such as the US Declaration of Independence (1776), where the rights of men were laid out succinctly (life, liberty, and the pursuit of happiness), perhaps for the first time (see Figure 6). By the 20th century, peace was a prominent motivation for liberal and radical political

IN CONGRESS, JULY 4, 1776.

A DECLARATION

BY THE REPRESENTATIVES OF THE

UNITED STATES OF AMERICA,

IN GENERAL CONGRESS ASSEMBLED.

6. The Declaration of Independence also brought to an end the war between the thirteen American colonies and Great Britain in 1776

and social thinkers, including Mahatma Gandhi and his ideas for non-violent civil resistance. Marxist understandings of class conflict and revolution leading to a communist utopia offer another vision of peace in a 'classless society', which has been influential. Alternatively, society may attain peace through pacifism and an aspiration to one or other spiritual order. Peace may rest on monolithic and closed political orders and their relations with other units (often seen as a communitarian form of politics), or on shared norms and identities and the coexistence of difference (cosmopolitanism).

The historical evolution of peace has shifted from a negative and narrow version to a positive and broad concept of peace. It has evolved across history as both an aspiration and a fact, emerging from any number of social movements, alliances and treaties, institutions, as well as in famous philosophical, political, social, and economic texts. The gradual adoption of this broader view has also allowed for a shift of the basis of peace from elite and state, or imperial interests, to those of society in everyday life, supported by a reformed state and evolving international system. This set the stage for the 20th century's various political, military, and social struggles.

# Chapter 3
# Peace in modernity

The international system in the 20th century was comprised of different versions of states, law, institutions, trade, constitutions, and civil society. Together, they came to represent an international architecture of peace thought to be progressive. Modern, liberal conceptions of peace are usually secular, and focus on security, political institutions, democracy and human rights, development, and trade, as the drivers of peace. They are promoted by many of the dominant peacebuilding actors, agencies, and states, such as the UN, World Bank, or key donors like the USA, UK, Japan, or the EU. This international peacebuilding architecture represents the apogee of a contemporary art or science of peace, along with a very powerful critique desiring social justice, implying much greater international equality is required.

## Peace into the 20th century

The emergence of conscientious objection during World War I was one of the best-known elements of what had become an anti-war stance. Conscientious objectors were often imprisoned by the state (in Britain's case) until pacifism became recognized as a legitimate concern of citizens, for whom civilian work could legally be a substitute for active military service. The process that led to this was strongly supported by Cambridge University philosopher Bertrand Russell (1872–1970), who was at various times a liberal, a socialist, and a pacifist, and was one of the most famous philosophers of his day. Campaigns for trade and disarmament were important, as in the writings of Norman Angell, a famous anti-war campaigner in the early 20th century (1872–1967). Both writers increased the popular appeal of these ideas.

Prominent businessmen of the era also became involved in promoting world peace, most famously Andrew Carnegie, who used his enormous wealth from the American steel industry in the early 20th century to support trusts and organizations engaged in peace work, as well as funding the construction of the Peace Palace at The Hague. This now houses the International Court of Justice among other institutions.

World War I was a great disruption for the various peace movements. However, after the Treaty of Versailles brought World War I to an end there emerged a discussion of the value of a liberal and democratic form of peace along with the foundation of the League of Nations. These were the basis for an attempt to build a positive peace. Peace henceforth was to include disarmament, institutions created to manage conflict, collective action, arbitration over disputes between states, and a Secretariat, as well as a Council whose role it was to enforce the peace. A High Commission for Refugees was created to deal with the acute post-war refugee problem. Another institution was to manage the colonial system, which was beginning to collapse. The treaty was shaped by US President Wilson's (1856–1924) 'Fourteen Points', which were intended to make the world 'safe for democracy' through consent rather than through domination or occupation. Wilson's Fourteen Points were remarkably similar to Kant's 'articles' for perpetual peace: there should be no secret agreements between countries; diplomacy and negotiation should be public; there should be free trade, and freedom of the seas; and there should be a general disarmament. However, the US Senate rejected the treaty and the USA did not join the

League, though Wilson received the Nobel Peace Prize in 1919 for his efforts.

The foundation of the International Labour Organization (ILO) in 1919 was partly a result of the activism of workers and a growing awareness of the importance of the concept of social justice. That the ILO became the first specialized agency of the UN in 1946 was a mark of its importance. It was subsequently to set international standards and regulate employee/employer relations in order to mitigate the exploitative dynamics that had so often led to civil conflict.

Even in the inter-war period, often viewed as the bleakest of epochs marked by financial and political crises, a World Disarmament Conference was convened in 1932. Several major peace movements continued to operate, including the British Peace Pledge Union, the Women's International League for Peace and Freedom, an American organization, War Resisters International, and various Quaker organizations.

Mahatma Gandhi introduced the approaches of *satyagraha* (truth) and *ahimsa* (non-violence), which combined a campaign for social justice, development, and equality with non-violence. He used these methods to undermine British colonialism in India, but they had a wider impact on the legitimacy of colonialism around the world, rebutting its claim to represent a 'civilizing mission' and exposing its often oppressive and racist character.

A notable post-war event reflected the rapid return and rise of tensions in Europe once again. In 1932, continuing and further endorsing a long-standing academic engagement with peace throughout history, Albert Einstein (1879–1955), well known for developing the general theory of relativity, and Sigmund Freud (1856–1939), the father of psychoanalysis, joined forces to add their intellectual credibility to the various peace movements with an article called 'Why War?' They debated the human capacity to avoid war. Freud wrote,

> How long shall we have to wait before the rest of mankind become pacifists too? There is no telling.... But one thing we can say: whatever fosters the growth of civilization works at the same time against war.

Einstein returned to the peace issue in 1955 when he published a manifesto with Bertrand Russell designed to prevent a nuclear conflict, calling on world leaders to seek peaceful solutions to international conflict. It exhorted its readers thus: '[w]e appeal, as human beings, to human beings: Remember your humanity and forget the rest.' Russell himself was later to associate the peace movement with an aim of creating a world government, as did H. G. Wells (1866–1946), a prolific English writer, socialist, pacifist, and campaigner on social issues.

In 1945, after the end of World War II, which was perhaps the greatest challenge to international peace ever posed, justice was pursued through an International Military Tribunal which the Allies formed to try Nazi war criminals at Nuremberg. Reconstruction of much of Western Europe was provided through the US Marshall Plan. The establishment of the UN system as well as the European Coal and Steel Community, and subsequently the European Economic Community, were aimed at providing an international and regional architecture to cement the new peace.

The Bandung Conference of 1955 in Indonesia, attended by twenty-nine newly independent states from the global south including India and Indonesia and representing nearly 1.5 billion people, began a political movement that saw itself as an alternative to the existing post-Cold War order and its inherent instability. In 1961, the Non-Aligned Movement formed, led by Yugoslavia, Indonesia, India, Egypt, and other states that wanted an alternative approach to politics and development. Briefly at least, it promoted the development of states in the global south as a counterweight to the dominant ideologies of the ongoing Cold War. New voices from the global south were now beginning to enter a debate about the nature of international order, until then mainly dominated by the empires and states of the global north. Social and transnational movements in the global north were also beginning to make themselves felt, campaigning on issues from disarmament to civil rights, apartheid, and other aspects of social justice.

The peace movement also attracted the attention of US President John F. Kennedy, who said in a speech in Washington in 1963:

> I speak of peace, therefore, as the necessary rational end of rational men . . . world peace, like community peace, does not require that each man love his neighbour—it requires only that they live together in mutual tolerance . . . our problems are man-made— therefore they can be solved by man.

During this period, UN peacekeeping emerged as a new tool to mitigate or prevent conflicts within and between states. It aimed primarily at preventing small conflicts from igniting a superpower conflict. During the period leading up to the collapse of the Soviet Union in 1989–90 both Mikhail Gorbachev, influenced by the Russell–Einstein Manifesto, and US President Ronald Reagan appeared to agree that nuclear wars could not be won and that significant conventional and non-conventional disarmament was required. The anti-nuclear movement had long argued for this cause.

## The liberal peace after the Cold War

After the collapse of the Soviet Union, the liberal peace became, for the West at least, the leading response to conflict, war, and violence. An awareness of the global, regional, state, and local dynamics of peace, and its social, economic, political, and cultural dimensions, had now coalesced around the benefits of democracy and capitalism, some social welfare on the part of the state, and an international architecture of peace and development led by the UN. UN Conventions, documents, committees, agencies, and organizations now began to develop and focus on improving the local, state, and global dynamics of social, political, economic, and institutional aspects of peace. The most important of these were *An Agenda for Peace* in 1992, the Cairo Population Summit of 1992, the Rio de Janeiro 'Earth Summit' of 1992, the Beijing Women's Summit of 1995, the UN Millennium Declaration of 2000, and *Responsibility to Protect* in 2005. These conferences established the modern parameters for peace.

Liberal, internationalist, idealist, and pacifist movements have been associated with humanitarianism, the formation of international institutions like the UN, international law, democracy, free trade, and forms of economic redistribution. They have also led to popular mobilization and to non-violent resistance as a method for their attainment.

Modern peace incorporates a diverse array of aspects. Once security is assured (a negative peace) the next stage is create a positive peace. Reducing arms and their trade (and especially nuclear weapons) has also been very important. The liberal peace has become the foundation of the modern international system of states and order (as opposed to peace through world government). Many organizations, which might be formerly thought of as agents of a more negative or victor's style peace (such as NATO), have also developed in this direction.

This period also saw the elevation of voices from the global south added to the chorus and activities relating to the reform of the old warlike (often patriarchal) sovereignties of empire or state. Long-standing, sometimes racist, patriarchal, and colonial understandings of peace, and even more sophisticated versions based on liberal internationalism, have gradually broadened.

Catastrophic wars occurred in the 20th century, of course, but their numbers dropped by the end of the century. War was becoming increasingly undermined as a political tool except where there were significant threats against the international community, or for humanitarian reasons, to overthrow occasional renegade and terrorist-supporting regimes, as in Bosnia, Sierra Leone, or Afghanistan and Iraq.

The UN continued to develop its capacity for peace along with the donor system. International law was increasingly taken seriously even if not enforced. Nuclear and other disarmament was widely discussed and became internationally accepted. Expectations about peace also now included issues relating to civil society, human rights, and extended into research and education. Policymaking on peace, development, security, rights, and needs has advanced significantly, even if the redress of direct or structural violence has so far been uneven. Concepts like human security (as opposed to state security) became part of the institutional agenda in the UN system in the 1990s, emphasizing the human consequences of conflict and dimensions of peace.

This has not been an unblemished record of accomplishment. Nevertheless, the capacity of the emerging international peace architecture, and international and social pressure for peaceful processes of politics and dispute settlement, has grown enormously. Direct and structural violence, proliferation, a lack of capacity in the UN, unsustainable development, poverty, gender inequality, and human trafficking continue. However, responses are gathering pace, and are increasingly built into law, institutions, politics, constitutions, policy, education, and social expectations.

Variations on the liberal peace are now also emerging, often supported by the newer players, such as the emerging countries and a range of local and transnational actors, on the world stage. The majority of states in the international community now appear to be relatively content (even if, like China and Russia, they are not liberal democracies) to allow the liberal peace to partly shape the status quo. However, they may still harbour some concerns about its specific characteristics or refuse to become involved in the reforms it requires (whilst supporting its economic prescriptions for capitalism). Most recognized states today play a role in various international organizations—from the UN to the IMF, World Bank, European Union, Organization for Security and Cooperation in Europe (OSCE), the African Union, and many other regional organizations—in the creation of the liberal peace in the many parts of today's world where war has occurred or still threatens.

At the elite or state level diplomats and international officials utilize negotiation, mediation, conflict resolution, peacebuilding, statebuilding, or development processes. International peacekeepers' military and humanitarian intervention may contribute. Peace processes now often involve the provision of significant support by international actors. A 'will to peace' in positive or even hybrid form is a local and international, collective aspiration, even if a 'will to power' (implying at best a negative peace) has often captured the world's headlines.

# Chapter 4
# The victors' peace in history

to the victor, the spoils.

Attributed to US Senator William Marcy, 1832

the nature of War consisteth not in actual fighting: but in
the known predisposition thereto, during all the time there
is no assurance to the contrary. All other time is Peace.

Thomas Hobbes, *Leviathan*

The victor's peace has evolved from the historical view that peace
emerges from a military victory. This form of negative peace is
coercive and often unjust but it may be orderly, for at least as long
as the victor survives. It may even provide the basis for a more
sophisticated version to emerge. It has long been thought to be the
oldest understanding of peace, foreshadowing the Darwinian
notion of the survival of the fittest and implying war and violence
was humanity's natural condition. In these terms, any limited
peace was merely an interlude until the next armed confrontation
over territory and resources arose. The continued domination of
the victor—often an empire, whether that of Alexander the Great,
the Romans, British, or vis-à-vis US influence today—meant the
peace it imposed was likely to survive any challenges, but for no
longer than its power lasted.

The model of peace implied by such a formulation is inherently limited, based upon military control or occupation, on colonialism or imperialism. At best it leads to a basic form of order created through domination, or alliances and a balance of power whereby states and leaders perceive war as too costly to win because of their opponent's strength. Such thinking is well described by the formulation of a 'negative peace'.

The Roman destruction of the city of Carthage (149 BC), which is in modern Tunisia, is probably the best-known and earliest example of the victor's peace. On the defeat of Carthage's armies Rome declared that the city of Carthage should be razed and its lands strewn with salt, thus attempting to remove it completely from the world map. Carthage has ironically been remembered precisely for this. A victor's peace needed more than force, however. It also needed law: the first emperor of the Babylonian empire placed stone tablets around his territories (c.1789 BC) outlining the terms of the peace in a 'Code of Laws', which he imposed after winning a war.

A victor's peace was discussed in a range of ancient sources. Thucydides (460–c.395 BC), a Greek historian and Athenian general, wrote about his experiences in his book *History of the Peloponnesian War*, between Sparta and Athens. Athens was, before the war, the most powerful city-state in Greece, but after a series of failed peace treaties with Sparta was eventually beaten. Sparta became the leading city-state in turn. The war had a devastating economic impact and undermined the idea of democracy that Athens promoted, replacing it with Sparta's authoritarian approach, and leading to repeated wars across the Hellenic world. Thucydides concluded that power determined international relations, though he also explored the problems for victims in the famous 'Melian Dialogue'. The Athenians stated that:

> the strong do what they can and the weak suffer what they must…it is not as if we were the first to make this law, or to act

upon it when made: we found it existing before us, and shall leave it to exist forever after us; all we do is to make use of it, knowing that you and everybody else, having the same power as we have, would do the same as we do.

A number of other historical sources laid out similar arguments and experiences. Sun Tzu, in his masterpiece of strategy *The Art of War* (c.476–221 BC), laid out how wars could be won whilst also advocating cooperation and diplomacy with other states. The latter were also significant in Augustine's *The City of God* (5th century AD). For him war was representative of the 'fallen condition' of humanity. Nevertheless, war could be legitimately fought against the enemies of Christendom. War within Christendom was sinful, and so should be carefully conducted. The 'city of god' would be a Christian empire of peace, though it might not be peaceful in its dealings with non-Christians. Machiavelli's seminal study *The Prince* (1513) pointed to the justification for using immoral means to achieve glory or survival. Thomas Hobbes's *Leviathan* (1651) claimed that a 'state of nature'—meaning 'war of all against all'—could only be prevented by strong central government to which society is subservient. Abuses of power are the price of peace. These arguments indicated that war and power dominated order, but also that important nuances were developing understanding of peace and war. They grappled with the problem of which takes precedence: power, survival, or norms? Do power and interests outweigh norms (meaning the powerful do what they want even if it undermines the rights and dignity of other people), and what may be a 'just' war for a just peace (meaning can war even be legitimate and be used to create a peace people may accept)? Paradoxically, sometimes war is conducted for reasons of achieving peace; sometimes peace is of exclusive benefit to one or other group. There are also less ambiguous arguments in the early literatures on peace and war, such as in the growing belief that injustice and deprivation were important stimuli for war.

Francisco de Vitoria, a Spanish Renaissance philosopher and jurist who wrote about just war, thought that the stage was being set for a new era of victor's peace: uninhabited lands were available for exploitation providing a reason for a victor's peace, which was justified as being in the interests of the prince.

While Hobbes's *Leviathan* argued that combating of the 'state of nature' mainly rested upon the interests and capacities of the 'Leviathan' (this was a reference to a large sea monster, by which Hobbes meant the most powerful actor), he was also aware of the need for consensus and legitimacy within society for any authority.

The colonial or imperial systems that arose from the power and interests of the European industrial states saw them take control of vast populations and swathes of land around the world for glory, profit, and to 'civilize the native'. This was a kind of victor's peace. The development of European colonialism and imperialism was predicated on the right of a superior race to dominate those whom it identified as lesser.

The British Empire's exploration of new sea routes during the Elizabethan era (1558–1603) led to a rapid realization of the potential for trade, and ultimately of the financial and military benefits of territorial acquisition and control. Implicit in this development was the relationship between war, trade, and peace in the colonies and dependencies. Peace was perceived as very different from the perspective of the occupier or the local inhabitants. By the end of the 19th century, European imperialism came to be characterized less by the exploitation of a territory's resources and inhabitants and more by a liberal 'civilizing mission' thought to benefit local inhabitants. Of course, this was often disguised by little more than a veneer of benevolence.

Massive industrialization had also amplified the capacity at the disposal of states and imperial powers to make war. Some states drifted towards fascism as demands grew ever greater for territory, material resources, and markets. The state was a vital component of this extreme attempt to amass power so war could be used as a political tool. According to such arguments, war might also provide a context in which individuals might demonstrate their capacity for an ethical life. In fact, peace for Hegel (1770–1831), a German philosopher who made similar arguments, would produce a 'corruption of nations'.

Given that a victor's peace is mainly dependent upon overwhelming power, which has been a rare historical occurrence, a compromise on this formulation emerged in the balance of power system that marked European politics for much of the 19th and early 20th century. This rested upon a system of alliances that maintained a negative peace between states and empires. The weakness of such a peace, as can be seen in early 20th century European history, is that it is susceptible to collapse. Alliances may maintain order but they may also be called upon for support against aggressive states as with Germany in 1914 and 1939. Such conflicts may quickly escalate into regional or world wars as alliance systems are triggered, and because of which the previous international system and its empires may collapse.

The outbreak of war in 1914 was greeted with a general incredulity that 'civilization' could still tolerate war. As the 'Great War's' associated direct and collateral costs mounted, it became clear that war had become an end in itself without any clear objectives or benefits. World War I showed for the first time that large-scale industrialized war could not be won decisively, even at great cost. Indeed, any victor's peace might be so costly that it would be meaningless.

The Versailles Settlement that followed was in some respects a victor's peace, in that its terms were determined by US President Wilson's 'Fourteen Points'. As Keynes foresaw in his book *The Economic Consequences of the Peace* (1919), World War I's victors forced the defeated Axis powers to accept terms that might lead to war restarting in the future. This illustrates both the aim of the victor's peace—to remove the threat of the defeated forever—as well as its weaknesses—that somehow, in fact or in legend, they may rise again. As the victor's power wanes, the latter becomes more likely.

Indeed, the European empires faded swiftly from the international stage after the end of World War I and World War II. These wars both drained their resources and strengthened local claims for self-determination in colonies around the world.

The victor's peace has historically rested on the argument that power can be exercised by the hegemon (meaning a state or empire that controls the most resources), driven by their imperial or strategic interests. However, war may be both waged and mitigated by their attempts to maintain order (perhaps softened by a colonial 'civilizing mission' designed to 'modernize' colonies as with the British Empire after the 1890s). The inter-war drift back to an acceptance of the legitimacy of a victor's peace was to have a decisive effect on 20th century history: not merely via its two industrial-scale world wars but more subtly on the peace architecture subsequently established after both world wars in the shape of the League of Nations and the United Nations system.

The creation of the League, the UN, and NATO reflected this tension. The North Atlantic Treaty Organization (NATO)—a military alliance based on the North Atlantic Treaty of 1949— represented a collective security system designed to maintain the new order on behalf of, at the most recent count, 28 member states across North America and Europe. An additional 22 countries are now involved in NATO's 'Partnership for Peace'. The membership of NATO accounts for approximately 70 per cent of the world's military budgets. NATO was politically involved in the Cold War struggle, and intervened militarily during the breakup of Yugoslavia in Bosnia in the mid-1990s and again in Kosovo in

1999, invoking a new doctrine of humanitarian intervention. NATO also perceived the 9/11 atrocities in New York as an attack on all its members and later became involved in Afghanistan through the NATO-led International Security Assistance Force. Recently, in 2011, it enforced a no-fly zone over Libya, following UN Security Council Resolution 1973. From 1990 the victor's peace became the basis for the liberal peace, as the pursuit of a victor's peace was gradually superseded by demands for a new form of positive peace in the minds of citizens around the world, who had seen the acute destruction war had brought.

## Beyond the victor's peace

Contemporary examples of the victor's peace include the case of Rwanda after the genocide of 1994. The current President, Paul Kagame, invaded the country and brought the genocide to an end, imposing a new state of affairs that has since pacified the country, though his government has been criticized on the grounds of human rights abuses. It could also be said that the NATO bombing campaigns in former Yugoslavia in 1995 in Bosnia-Herzegovina or 1999 in Kosovo, as well as Belgrade, both aimed against Serb forces, or the invasions of Afghanistan and Iraq in the 2000s, also represented a contemporary version of a victor's peace. All of these cases also provided the basis for an attempt to create viable liberal democracies in these countries, however.

The victor's peace framework has many flaws: it is subject to the problem of territorial and strategic over-extension, and an inability to control 'unruly' subjects. In particular, hegemonic powers are often surprised by local resistance to their rule. This may be internally, as with much of the resistance to the control of the Soviet Union (the Prague Spring in 1968, the Polish resistance to their own government in the 1980s, or the collapse of the Berlin Wall in 1989). Or it may be externally, as with Indian resistance to the British Empire in the early 20th century during the independence campaign or the continuing attacks against US and other foreign targets in the ongoing 'statebuilding' mission in Afghanistan. The same is true in the case of resistance against US occupation in Vietnam or Iraq in the 1960s and 2000s respectively, or against the ongoing Israeli occupation of Palestine.

Such resistance often occurs despite the overwhelming military power the hegemon or victor can bring to bear. It indicates one of the curious paradoxes of the victor's peace and the particular brand of political realism (in practice and theory) that it emanates from: that power, however overwhelming in military, financial, political, or even normative terms, never quite seems to be enough to quell the local desire for autonomy, self-determination, and a positive form of peace. A lesson of history is that local consent and legitimacy are eventually needed for any victor's peace to be maintained and for it to advance into a more sophisticated form, meaning that its coercive character begins to weaken. Ironically a victor's peace may then collapse if the hegemonic power loses interest in maintaining it or if resistance to it is widespread.

# Chapter 5
# The constitutional peace

Despite the apparent prevalence of the victor's peace throughout history much of the historical record also points to the legitimacy of broader understandings of peace. The idea that peace could be constructed through law, institutions, rights, and prosperity, rather than enforced or merely preserved by military power, emerged slowly during and after the Enlightenment as an advance on the victor's peace. This was partly in response to violent excesses of elite and state power, and partly to satisfy growing mobilization for a range of rights from within society.

The post-Enlightenment period was the platform for a struggle to achieve a more sophisticated version of peace than any victory in war might allow for. This order was to be more stable than one dependent solely on victory in a conflict, and was gradually seen to be founded upon the creation of both a domestic political and legal architecture and an international architecture designed to balance the interests, needs, and rights of the population. It would have the significant benefit of making the international order more sustainable because it would be based upon a positive peace.

This domestic political architecture may be called the constitutional peace. It has been debated since Plato, Pericles, and Aristotle's discussions of the 'good life', and the merits of democracy versus the role of philosopher kings in ancient Greece.

The theme of what shape good government should take emerged again during the Enlightenment in northern Europe. With the Treaty of Westphalia in 1648 it was realized that peace was related to the form the state should take, which should enable it to become a peaceful and accepted member of a stable international order, while also benefiting its population.

## Perpetual peace and liberal constitutions

As the Enlightenment progressed the Hobbesian view that war was part of the natural fabric of international life, manipulated by Machiavellian princes, was displaced. Leaders, scholars, and general populations began to argue that peace should be central to political life and institutions. Peace was achievable rather than merely an ideal to be aspired to—and this should be thought about in the context of nation-states. Renaissance humanism (which developed during the 14th and 15th centuries AD) emphasized the need for a citizenry, including women, to engage in civic life in the state and follow virtuous courses of action. The liberalism that subsequently emerged challenged the idea that violence and war were part of the natural order of things. Peace could be the product of human ingenuity, especially if states and leaders could be sufficiently engaged. Enlightened actors with liberal views and objectives could now mitigate war.

Another important contribution was the historical argument that 'just war' should be waged by a legitimate authority only as a last resort and in response to an act of unjustified aggression. This had two effects: one, a growing concern with the nature of the type of state that would be more conducive to peace, and two, an interest in international organization and institutions designed to create and maintain peace. The constant religious wars of that era in Europe were eventually brought to an end by an agreement along these lines, involving territorial states whose sovereignty might not be violated by other states. The implications were that territorial states and their international arrangements were necessary for a peace built either on common values or on an agreement to differ. Thus, the understanding of peace developed into a balance of power between states, guaranteed through international treaties and alliances, as was endorsed by the Treaty of Westphalia in 1648.

Soon after, John Locke argued that a law-based government would produce consensus, legitimacy, and therefore a domestic peace. A social contract was required in order to cement a consensual and representative relationship between leaders and society, the state providing security and acting as a 'neutral judge' to protect the lives, liberty, and property of citizens.

Free trade was an important component of the constitutional peace. Adam Smith's *Wealth of Nations* (1776) argued that international trade should be the basis of cooperation, prosperity, and peace between and within states.

Kant, in his book *Perpetual Peace*, based his subsequent understanding of peace upon the creation of just laws that would be reflected in a 'republican' or democratic political order. These conditions would crucially also prevent war between states. *Perpetual Peace* laid out the conditions through which an early form of social justice could be attained within states and peace could be achieved between states (later to be reflected in the UN Charter in 1945).

Kant's *Perpetual Peace* was probably the most comprehensive statement until then of how to bring peace to a Europe that was constantly in turmoil. These arguments gave rise to what has now become known as the liberal democratic peace thesis, for which a huge literature has constructed an argument that supports democratization. Its modern version states that democratic states do not go to war with each other, though they might fight non-democracies. Kant wrote:

> [I]f the consent of the citizens is required in order to decide that war should be declared (and in this constitution it cannot but be the

case), nothing is more natural than that they would be very cautious in commencing such a poor game, decreeing for themselves all the calamities of war. Among the latter would be: having to fight, having to pay the costs of war from their own resources, having painfully to repair the devastation war leaves behind, and, to fill up the measure of evils, load themselves with a heavy national debt that would embitter peace itself and that can never be liquidated on account of constant wars in the future.

Following these constitutional strands of thinking about peace and order, Jeremy Bentham (1748–1832), a British philosopher and social reformer, added a concern with a number of social issues: welfare, economic freedom, the separation of church and state, freedom of expression, equal rights for women, and the abolition of slavery and the death penalty. He offered the utilitarian insight for government that the greatest happiness for the greatest good would lead to peace, as the British economist David Ricardo (1772–1823) confirmed in an economic sense. Despite the criticism from British economist Thomas Malthus (1766–1834), who believed that surplus populations would lead to unsustainable development, resource depletion, and war, the free trade argument continued to be an essential pillar of the emerging version of peace. However, it was propagated through an uncomfortable mixture of British liberalism and colonialism until the early 20th century.

Liberal thinking was beginning to crystallize into more than speculation: John Stuart Mill (1806–73), a British philosopher, connected development with peace, individual liberty, and private property. He claimed that peace lay in both the protection of individual freedoms and the existence of effective government.

## Limitations of perpetual peace

According to the constitutional peace, peace would be constructed through consensual processes so that society would accept its legitimacy. Finding the balance between a Leviathan and the population's interests has been a difficult task. The problem with Kant's assumption that states act to maximize the interests of their own peoples (where they treat them as means rather than ends) is that states and elites may exploit their people instead. The line between contributing to peace or following a nationalist or elite interest was, and is, finely drawn.

The emergence of nationalism was also a consequence of what John Stuart Mill identified as the right of people to determine their own government. This may mean pursuing a national interest and identity not necessarily commensurate with regional or international peace or universal norms. As the principle of national self-determination gained popular appeal in the last 100 or so years, especially during the dissolution of the Ottoman and Austro-Hungarian, French, British, and other European empires after World War I and World War II, and at the end of the Cold War (in the Balkans for example), the concepts of both nationalism and ethno-nationalism became associated with the foundations not of order but of war. This soon became a spark for war between groups laying claim to the same territory. It continues to do so in the contemporary era, as the cases of Cyprus, Sudan, Bosnia-Herzegovina, Israel/Palestine, and others suggest.

Another concern has been that the constitutional peace has been characterized as a Christian enterprise, even if it is supposed to be secular. The peace plans had the objective of stabilizing Europe, since the Treaty of Westphalia was essentially based upon Christian ethics and a balance between cosmopolitan and communitarian thought.

Nevertheless, the democratic or liberal peace argument does seem to have held. One of the most significant exceptions has been that democracies may still fight wars against non-democracies, for a range of reasons, as the cases of military intervention in Afghanistan and Iraq in the early 2000s have shown. The democratic peace assumes states will evolve into democracies. Because this has often not been the case, and many states continued to fight wars or infringed their citizens' human rights, the constitutional peace has proven to be inadequate. It was hoped by Kant and other great thinkers of his era that an international organization aimed at promoting human rights and democracy and keeping the peace would resolve this problem.

The constitutional peace is focused on an elite-level official discourse by state and government, and geographically and temporally bounded by sovereign statehood. All of this is mitigated by its attempt to promote a liberal framework of government for the state, but the constitutional peace project continues to be underpinned by the use of force. However, it remains one of the only 'laws' of international relations. Since the end of the Cold War it has been defined by democracy, free trade, and human rights, as Francis Fukuyama notably described in his essay 'The End of History and the Last Man' (1989), which celebrated the potential for the spread of democracy after the end of the Cold War.

The liberal-democratic peace thesis is firmly embedded in the current international architecture of peace, in many states' constitutions, international law, the role of donors, the UN, International Nongovernmental Organizations (INGOs), and International Financial Institutions (IFIs) like the World Bank. As a result, many of the world's states today have liberal-democratic institutions and constitutions (63% according to Freedom House in 2013), which also involve a commitment to human rights. It is notable that the European Union today owes a great deal of its constitutional structure to the Enlightenment peace projects, which promoted the constitutional peace.

This thinking shaped the frontier of knowledge after the end of the Cold War about what necessary components any state should include in its constitution if it is to remain peaceful. Several states went even further during the last century in their pursuit of peace:

according to German Basic Law, Germany is not allowed to have offensive armed forces (a relic of Allied occupation after World War II); Japan (at least until recently) is said likewise to have a 'peace constitution', and other countries like Costa Rica have completely dismantled their armed forces.

As a caveat, Kant once remarked that the *perpetual peace* he envisaged might turn out to be rather unpleasant, and Fukuyama repeated this warning. Liberal democracy and free trade seem to have become the only viable form of politics and peace after the end of the Cold War, but incessant materialism and the related consumption of raw materials might ultimately lead to a hollow victory and even to environmental collapse. In practice the application of the constitutional peace has often been blocked by actors who do not want to share power and who oppose domestic legal structures that might outlaw their authoritarian or corrupt activities. This has not changed since Hitler and Mussolini ignored the League of Nations in the 1920s and 1930s, or when Saddam Hussein ignored the UN over his invasion of Kuwait in the 1990s and blocked inspections of his possible weapons of mass destruction programme in the early 2000s.

# Chapter 6
# The institutional peace

...till the war-drum throbb'd no longer, and the battle-flags
were furl'd,
In the Parliament of man, the Federation of the World.
    Alfred, Lord Tennyson, 'Locksley Hall', 1837–8

The 19th century English poet Alfred, Lord Tennyson (1809–92)
lauded the potential of international cooperation and law (as well
as making an implicit reference to democracy), as in the quotation
above. He pointed to a third form of peace that has been very
influential in the modern era. The role of international institutions
and law in supporting the consolidation of a constitutional peace
within and between states represents the next step in building a
positive peace. The institutional peace began to develop around the
same time as the constitutional peace became prominent, during
the Enlightenment. By the second half of the 20th century the UN,
international donors, international law, and a range of regional
actors, notably the EU and the African Union, coalesced around a
more dynamic approach with the aim of creating a wide-ranging
positive peace. The constitutional peace provides a direct link
between the development of an international architecture to
maintain peace between states and the liberal democratic peace.

The institutional peace aims to anchor states within a specific set
of values and a shared legal context through which they agree

multilaterally how to behave. They also agree to police and enforce that behaviour on the part of 'renegade' states. Before the era of states, kings and queens tried to achieve this through alliances, peace treaties, marriages, trusteeships, and other forms of political relationship. Alexander the Great (356–323 BC) used many of these techniques to hold together his expanding empire. Two millennia later, the leaders of the emerging states in Europe began to institutionalize recurrent high-level diplomatic conferences. These were often held to debate matters of war and peace and so were perceived as a way out of the cycles of violence that the victor's peace had given rise to.

An emerging set of intentional institutions created to cement a stable international order was complementary to the growing belief that liberal democratic states were less likely to go to war with each other. If states have democratic constitutions and share common goals of peace and free trade, they may organize themselves into an international community. An international 'peace architecture' was beginning to develop through which states would agree about and follow international norms and international law.

## The early development of international institutions

The institutional peace is part of a cosmopolitan ethic dating back to Diogenes the Cynic (c.412–323 BC), who declared himself a cosmopolitan. This idea posited that despite people's many differences a universally shared morality as well as international cooperation was possible, and that a world government might eventually be desirable. It found its contemporary character in the peace project associated with the Enlightenment. The Grotian discourse on natural law also made an important contribution. Natural law is based upon coexistence and non-intervention and states have a right of self-defence, following 'just war' thinking.

The Abbé de Saint-Pierre (1658–1743), an influential French writer, proposed in his book *Project for Perpetual Peace* (1713) an international organization responsible for maintaining peace. This was the start of a formal Enlightenment genre of peace projects, spurring Kant and others to develop these ideas further in the face of continuing European wars. Saint-Pierre's peace plan was essentially a European treaty for a federation of states, in which law would be founded upon justice, equality, and reciprocity. Saint-Pierre called for the Christian (and also Muslim) sovereigns of Europe to form a permanent union for peace and security. This organization would not intervene in the affairs of member states but would have intelligence and self-defence capacities and might even send in troops to preserve peace. William Penn also wanted to see a form of European parliament, in order to achieve 'peace with justice'.

Once again, Kant made an important contribution. He insisted that the rule of law envisaged by the democratic, constitutional peace he had argued for should be extended to international relations. This fell short of the establishment of a world government, but instead suggested a multilateral system of states:

> Reason would drive [states] to give up their savage lawless freedom, to accommodate themselves to public coercive laws, and thus to form an ever-growing State of Nations, such as would at last embrace all the Nations of the Earth. But as the Nations, according to their ideas of international Right, will not have such a positive rational system, and consequently reject in fact what is right in theory, it cannot be realised in this pure form. Hence, instead of the positive idea of a Universal Republic—if all is not to be lost—we shall have as result only the negative surrogate of a Federation of the States averting war, subsisting in an external union, and always extending itself over the world. (Kant, *Perpetual Peace*)

This has been a controversial issue faced by the institutional peace: whether to remain a multilateral system of states or to move towards a world government. Kant feared that a world government would be as unpleasant as a Hobbesian world as it might culminate in worse despotism. Thus, *Perpetual Peace* eventually finds itself reflected in the UN Charter, but as Kant specified, international order rests at best on a federation of free states. These should abolish war amongst themselves and offer non-citizens 'universal hospitality'. International trade would also be beneficial.

The Treaty of Westphalia (1648) is often taken to be the first point in modern history when the states-system began to emerge. This provided an impetus for international organizations to maintain peace between states. The Congress of Vienna in 1815 saw a system of international institutions begin to become a reality. Both helped to construct a framework that would support a peace that would stand in contrast to the wars that had gone before. The Congress of Vienna represented the attempt of statesmen such as Metternich, Castlereagh, and Talleyrand to create a realist balance of power which, however, depended upon their capacity to intervene in the affairs of other states. It was primarily an instrument of British 'order creation' and thus was very close to also being a victor's peace. This illustrates how closely the practice of peacemaking is often related to having power.

However, these developments were indicative of a rejection of the idea that war was endemic and inevitable. The conservatives and liberals of this era saw peace and war in different ways. The conservatives believed that peace lay in the preservation of the existing order, perhaps through the use of war, and certainly through a class system. Liberals believed that peace would be achieved through a transformation brought about by economic and social progress, for which war was an unwanted obstacle. Nationalists formed a third grouping, believing that nations had a right to self-determination, through the use of force if necessary.

Peace in 19th century Europe was disrupted by the growing forces of nationalism and by the constant imperial and colonial conflicts fought in North America, Asia, and Africa in search of an empire to glorify nationalism, to preserve the wealth of the old conservative order, and as a civilizing mission for liberals. Industrialization was by now making the scale of war greater and far more deadly than ever before. The formation of an international community intended to prevent war gathered pace almost simultaneously.

Disparate reforms and dynamics assisted the emergence of the institutional peace. Disarmament and rights campaigns often largely run from within civil society along with state-run humanitarian campaigns began to coalesce. For example, from 1816 to the 1860s Britain deployed a naval squadron against slave trading on the west coast of Africa. This reversal in the British approach to slavery meant a reinterpretation of international law to allow vessels to be boarded and searched. For the first time, perhaps, a humanitarian principle took precedence over the interests of the powerful, which would henceforth be crucial for the emerging set of international institutions.

Another dimension was provided by Henri Dunant's work leading to the Geneva Convention of 1864, and the creation of the International Committee of the Red Cross (ICRC) gave rise to what is now known as international humanitarian law. The ICRC is the oldest humanitarian organization, and is charged with the mandate (through international treaty) of being the custodian of the laws of war.

By the turn of the century, liberal internationalism appeared to be gathering pace. Major peace conferences were held at The Hague in 1899 and 1907, which also led to the eventual establishment of the Permanent International Court of Justice in 1922. In 1910 a Universal Peace Congress examined the need for international law, self-determination, and an end to colonialism. In 1913, another disarmament congress followed to mark the opening of

the Peace Palace in The Hague, funded by the American
industrialist Andrew Carnegie.

## The institutional peace after World War I

The institutional peace framework gained its most sophisticated
apparatus after the world wars of the 20th century. US President
Wilson's 'Fourteen Points' presented at the Versailles peace talks
after World War I were foundational in the emergence of a
modern notion of peace with both institutional and constitutional
dimensions. He called for the foundation of the League of Nations
to guarantee the sovereignty and territorial integrity of all states.
The League was to be an international mechanism of conflict
management that should prevent war for the successor states of
many of the now collapsing empires which had emerged as newly
democratized.

The post-World War I settlement was guided by the principle that
territorial adjustments should be of benefit to the populations
concerned—in other words, self-determination. Wilson believed
that this represented a peace without victory: yet it also
represented a unilateral American pronouncement, reminiscent of
the concept of the victor's peace, but more sophisticated. The
Versailles Treaty accentuated democratization within a state
framework, and regulated interstate relations, thus combining a
constitutional and institutional framework for peace. President
Wilson had in mind an 'ultimate peace of the world' reminiscent
of Kant's perpetual peace. It was to rest on a 'community of power'
and represented an 'organised common peace'. It was to be a
'peace without victory, a peace among equals'. Wilson told the US
Congress early in April 1917 that the 'world must be made safe for
democracy'. Perhaps most importantly a form of social justice was
now being seen as essential to a universal peace.

As it transpired Versailles was regarded as a victor's peace, and
this was its fatal flaw. This was exactly the fear underlying

John Maynard Keynes's famous critique of the Versailles settlement, specifically of the War Guilt Clause (Article 231) which blamed Germany for aggression, and of reparations to be paid by Germany. The way in which the Allies had established agreements while applying blame and financial responsibility to Germany and her allies meant that there would not be a stable peace resulting from the Treaty. German democracy would be 'annihilated' in the very process of trying to construct it. Some commentators, like E. H. Carr, who was a British delegate at the Versailles conference, believed the emerging institutional peace to be utopian and implausible.

There were also other competing versions of 'peace' emerging in the post-war order. One version was based upon the notion of a historical dialectic of progress and a classless society. Others derived from imperialism and nationalism. The major obstacle to Wilson's peace was that no state was prepared to take responsibility or provide guarantees for it. The US Congress did not want to be responsible at this level; Britain, France, and Germany still harboured their antipathies to each other; some statesmen and politicians still sought to justify imperialism and colonialism; Soviet Russia was concerned with its own revolution; militant nationalism was on the rise in Japan and elsewhere; and the collapse of the Ottoman and Austro-Hungarian Empires had left significant spoils to be fought over. The peace that had been created at Versailles was deeply flawed in practice, and was made even more fragile by the financial crises of the late 1920s that created socio-economic difficulty at a time when radical ideologies were making themselves widely felt.

## An international architecture for peace after World War II

The next attempt to create an institutional peace saw some of the lessons of the previous epoch applied or promptly forgotten. There were early signs even before World War II began. The new peace that was to follow the war was principally developed according to an American consensus. Cordell Hull (1871–1955), the longest-serving US Secretary of State for President Roosevelt, who received the Nobel Peace Prize in 1945 for his role in establishing the United Nations, introduced a Reciprocal Trade Act in 1934 to open up international trade as a counter to economic nationalism. This was reflected in the Atlantic Charter of 1941 signed by British Prime Minister Winston Churchill and US President Roosevelt, which laid out the internationalist case for cooperation, free trade, self-determination, decolonization, and the disarmament of aggressive states.

The new peace settlement was based upon a fragile framework spanning the UN Charter, the emerging Cold War confrontation between the USA and the USSR, and the creation of security, political, and economic arrangements between the USA, the Western industrial countries, and Japan. This new system included a military settlement and an institutional framework. It was developed by a mixture of public and private approaches and organizations, including the US Commission to Study the Basis of a Just and Durable Peace, and the Council for Foreign Affairs, and Britain's Chatham House.

The 'idealist' peace engendered in Wilsonianism, offering a positive and liberal peace framework after World War II, was now becoming firmly institutionalized in organizations and institutions that would constantly work to provide military security, legal guarantees, political consensus, humanitarian resources, and development and financial investment. The UN system that was now coming into being provided, via an alphabet soup of acronyms, an architecture for the institutional peace. It was formalized at the conferences of Dumbarton Oaks in 1944 and San Francisco in 1945. Peace came to engender the rejection of interstate war, the provision of humanitarian resources, development, financial regulation and adjustment, and human rights. Though the Security Council was its primary security organization, the UN's specialized agencies, funds, and programmes suggested a much broader view of peace. This meant that the World Health Organization, the International Labour Organization, the Food and Agriculture Organization, the UN Development Programme, the World Food Programme, the UN International Children's Emergency Fund, among others, were functional organizations established in order to create peace resting on social justice for citizens and ordinary people. The UN system did not evolve only from the liberal attempt to moderate the victor's peace and its underpinning political realism, but also as a response to the legitimate challenges that had been made in society for social justice, both at a material and ideological level.

It was from this growing network of ideas, concepts, and actors, engaging in a debate about how peace could henceforth be maintained in all of its local, state, and international aspects, that the notion of 'global governance' began to emerge as a concrete approach to institutionalizing the liberal peace across the planet. Perhaps the most notable statement on peace during this period was Roosevelt's belief that the American Senate's rejection of Wilson's peace in 1920 had been mistaken, and that there was now no turning back from the construction of a liberal international order of democratic states, open markets, and international cooperation. In this order there would be no place for formal imperialism or colonialism.

The International Military Tribunal, set up by the Allies in 1945 to try Nazi war criminals at Nuremberg, provided another important strand of the international architecture of peace. The tribunal had three main jurisdictions, one of which was 'crimes against peace'. Crimes against humanity and war crimes were the most recognized of its jurisdictions, however. The Allies defined a crime against peace as one that involved planning, preparing, or initiating an aggressive war. This soon led to a new wave of legal development with respect to crimes against humanity.

The new peace system was further buttressed by both security guarantees and economic redistribution. NATO played an important military (if only mainly symbolic) role in ensuring that the post-war system would be sustained by a collective security framework (though its capacity to oppose the military power of the Soviet Union was always somewhat questionable). The Truman Doctrine, designed to contain communism in Turkey and Greece, was US President Harry Truman's attempt, from 1947, 'to support free people who are resisting attempted subjugation by armed minorities or by outside pressures'. Marshall Aid (1948–52), a massive American programme named after US Secretary of State George Marshall, was intended to rebuild Europe and prevent the spread of communism.

This latter aspect of the new peace, however, was decidedly different in character. Where the emergence of a society of states seemed to signify a form of liberal peace, the 'containment order' which emerged as part of the 1947 Truman Doctrine indicated that there were large parts of the world which would be subject to a more traditional and limited negative concept of peace. They would effectively be isolated from the liberal peace both through Western policy and through their compliance with the regime of the USSR.

The Declaration of Human Rights in 1947, lobbied for by Eleanor Roosevelt, rapidly became a cornerstone of new thinking and policies for peace. The human rights discourse was derived especially from the work of Western thinkers such as Locke and Mill who put forward the view that individuals have an innate set of rights within the liberal tradition. Implicitly, human rights and peace are equated in much of the literature: one cannot exist without the other. This allowed the UN to base its work on a widely agreed set of standards that would henceforth underpin aspirations for a more sophisticated form of peace to emerge after World War II, further refined by the 1966 *Covenant on Economic, Social and Cultural Rights*. This also illustrated the influence of more critical thinking about peace and development from the political left and a range of post-colonial scholars who were by now arguing that the international system required a radical restructuring if inequality and structural violence were to be ended and social justice achieved.

Another contribution of this era to a more sophisticated and positive notion of peace which cemented the institutional framework for peace came from the Geneva Conventions (1949). These extended the earlier treaty in 1864 that established the International Red Cross, and established standards for international law pertaining to humanitarianism in wartime, the treatment of prisoners, the wounded, and the protection of civilians.

Indeed, international law has been crucial for the institutional peace framework as a set of binding rules between states that provides a stable international order. The new International Court of Justice, established by the UN Charter in 1945, later the European Court of Human Rights, established on the basis of the Council of Europe's 1950 European Convention on Human Rights, and the International Criminal Court, created by the Rome Statute in 2002, are the results of the evolving institutional peace framework. The development of consent-based governance frameworks at the international and national levels has now produced a significant array of norms, laws, and instruments for peace and justice. In terms of the institutional peace, the body of law about the conduct of war, international humanitarian law, and international human rights law, while slow, cumbersome, and sometimes unenforceable because states have to agree on a direct course of action, has been particularly significant.

A regional architecture for peace has also been vital to the emerging international architecture. The EU has emerged from a post-war attempt to pacify the relationship between the main European states, move away from nationalism, pool resources, and create common goals, and later began to harmonize trade, law, diplomacy, and foreign policy. In 1952 the European Coal and Steel Community was created as the first step towards a European federation, followed by the 1957 Treaty of Rome, which created the European Economic Community and a customs union. The now European Union has expanded to include twenty-eight countries, making it certainly the biggest and most successful regional attempt to maintain peace and order so far. It is a sophisticated successful example of regional conflict resolution and transformation.

Similarly, a network of other regional organizations is emerging around the world, perhaps most notably the African Union. It was established in 2001 as a successor to the Organization of African Unity (established in 1963), based in Addis Ababa, and consists of fifty-four African states. It aims at promoting solidarity between African countries and peoples, assisting in political and socio-economic integration and cooperation, as well as supporting security, democracy, human rights, and development.

# Chapter 7
# The civil peace

The next (and possibly most important) strand of the evolution of
the understanding of peace is the civil peace. According to this
approach, every individual in society has the capacity to mobilize
for peace from a variety of different perspectives, whether for
disarmament, for international cooperation, or against violence,
discrimination, and oppression. It relates to the historical
phenomena of social direct action for political, economic, and
identity reasons, of citizen advocacy and mobilization, in the
attainment or defence of basic human rights and values. It is also
related to pacifism in its main forms, where civil action is
non-violent in principle. It has been strongly influenced by a wide
range of social mobilization dynamics. Without the civil peace and
its social forms of mobilization, international and constitutional
frameworks would not be able to connect with ordinary people in
order to represent their interests, identities, needs, and
aspirations.

The civil peace often arises from localized organizations and their
campaigns, which are normally connected transnationally to other
similar movements around the world. Civil society develops as
local organizations, communities, and political actors coalesce
around the various dynamics and requirements of social justice.
It has often represented a direct and open challenge to structural
and direct violence embedded in the hierarchies of the state

system or within society itself (i.e. a negative peace). It was crucial in the late 19th and early 20th centuries when civil campaigns against slavery, for the vote, welfare, disarmament, and for women's enfranchisement had a very significant impact on the nature of the state and who was represented or who controlled politics legitimately.

## Civil society and peace: agency and mobilization

Social and advocacy movements began to emerge on a large scale during the 19th and 20th centuries. Two distinct pathways can be observed, including secular or religious orientations. They may have been derived from the secular emergence of liberal internationalism, associated with campaigns against conscription, ideological and feminist movements against war and for conventional disarmament, the campaign for nuclear disarmament, and environmental movements. Many resistance movements have also described themselves as peace movements, whether they were resisting authoritarian or colonial rule.

It is also important to note the significance of the American Revolution, which from 1774 rejected European aristocratic forms of leadership, in favour of republicanism and liberalism, and the French Revolutions from 1789, which saw the monarchy replaced by popular mobilization for similar principles of equality, citizenship, democracy, secularism, and basic human rights. These revolutions sought to devolve power to the population away from the lineage of royalty or colonialism, to attain personal freedom and representative government. Consequently, in the light of the realization of the potential of the political role of the individual and the possibilities of mass mobilization, often in non-violent ways, non-state actors began to gain a significant political role. This was not just by campaigning for more rights but also in responding to conflict, specifically in the context of human rights, multiple forms of discrimination, and humanitarian assistance.

Momentum grew in the 19th century through the creation of the International Committee of the Red Cross (ICRC), the mobilization of various social justice oriented movements, the abolition of the slave trade by the English Parliament in 1807, the campaigns for and introduction of voting rights for women (which began first in Sweden in 1718), the development of international law, and the growing popularity of disarmament campaigns. Many other activities organized by non-state actors were aimed at political, social, and economic reform.

Pacifist movements are sometimes related also to various long-standing peace churches, notably the Quaker and Mennonite movements, dating back to the 16th century. They have made an important contribution, as have public debates about non-violent resistance, the actions of conscientious objectors, civil disobedience, and even various forms of anarchism, especially in the 20th century. These dynamics formed an important strand of the evolving debate on how the civil peace could be achieved.

As international humanitarian law gradually influenced the state's understanding of war, this reinforced a more inclusive discourse of peace within the international system. By the 20th century, individuals had begun to lobby elites, leaders, and officials for peace in an organized manner. Partly because of such mobilization, The Hague peace conferences of 1899 and 1907, the International Court of Justice, and the 1910 and 1913 Universal Peace Congresses all pointed to the need for international law, self-determination, and an end to colonialism. Non-state actors were directly involved with the International Labour Organization from its establishment, and though they were excluded from The Hague Conferences in 1899 and 1907, their very exclusion was also an acknowledgement of their significance. Later, the League of Nations also provided non-state actors with informal consultative status. Such developments illustrate that there was a realization that peace could only be constructed if civil society was directly involved.

Such organizations soon began to proliferate: the International Rescue Committee (IRC) began its life rescuing Jews from Europe during World War II, and was later to be involved with retrieving Hungarian refugees after the failure of the 1956 uprising and Cuban refugees after Fidel Castro came to power in Cuba in 1959. Other such organizations followed, including the Catholic Relief Service, World Vision, and the Oxford Committee for Famine Relief (OXFAM).

Such efforts put positive forms of peace at the forefront of international and academic thinking. There was a growing recognition of the requirement of social justice for individuals and communities, and not just treaties or disarmament for or between states if peace was to be both just and sustainable. These were beginning to uncover the more subtle forms of power that blocked peace. These forms include bias towards hegemonic or elite interests, or towards the state or markets over society. They influenced the way power was exercised, the nature of the state and international community, and so the form of peace that was coming into being.

This view of a positive peace for civil society had an impact on the international system too. The Non-Aligned Movement, for example, wanted to propose an alternative approach to politics and development during the Cold War. This view was quietly influential, and the movement now includes nearly two-thirds of the UN's member states.

## The growing role of NGOs

Non-governmental organizations played an important role in highlighting the need for human rights to be included in the UN Charter at San Francisco in 1945, and helped draft the Universal Declaration of Human Rights. They have been significant in advocating for, and drafting, different UN treaties and conventions spanning issues from the elimination of discrimination against women (1979) to the rights of children (1989). They have played important roles in many other human rights-related UN working groups, as well as in the creation of the position of the UN High Commissioner for Human Rights.

Humanitarian law provides the legal context in which NGOs operate. One of the key early examples of contemporary humanitarianism was the Biafra crisis of 1968, when the Igbo people attempted to secede from Nigeria, causing the Nigerian Civil War. Despite their challenge to the sovereignty of Nigeria during this crisis, humanitarian aid NGOs mobilized regardless of international disapproval. This was repeated several times during the 1970s, in various crises in Bangladesh, Ethiopia, and Cambodia. Civil societies and NGOs were beginning to mobilize around the world to advocate for human rights, democracy, and emergency humanitarian assistance for the victims of war.

From these strands developed a powerful body of actors, and a development of a language of rights and norms that undermined the absolutism of Westphalian sovereignty and reinforced the view that individuals had legitimate rights for security, basic needs, autonomy, and to their own identity. International organizations and NGOS might intervene if states proved unable or unwilling to protect their own citizens.

There are now so many NGOs around the world it is almost impossible to count them, especially those local NGOs working in post-conflict and development contexts. The most familiar international NGOs working on peacebuilding and human rights include International Crisis Group, International Alert, Amnesty International, and Human Rights Watch. Amnesty International, for example, was founded in 1961, part of the huge international human rights movement that was emerging. The Helsinki Final Act reflected the growth of civil society movements, NGOs, and the support of human rights in 1975.

Many NGOs formed in the 1990s as a response to the broad requirements of the synthesis of peacebuilding, humanitarianism, human rights monitoring, and advocacy. They were to support a burgeoning civil society in post-conflict zones, which would then form the basis for a social contract and the liberal peace. It was partly because of civil society activism for human rights that humanitarian intervention emerged, meaning that states may now intervene in the affairs of other states for humanitarian reasons.

Organizations like ICRC, Médecins Sans Frontières (MSF), and the International Crisis Group (ICG), among many others, have also played an important role in other aspects of civil society, development, and assistance. NGOs are now a recognized part of the UN system, hold consultative status within the United Nations' platform on economic and social issues ECOSOC, and are an integral part of the humanitarian discourse. Under Article 71 of the UN Charter, ECOSOC is empowered to consult with NGOs on economic and social issues, as well as on matters relating to refugees, the environment, and development. This is particularly important in the context of debates about human security and the emergence of a 'global civil society', meaning that there is solidarity across the world's societies which may support peace and security where states fail.

However, humanitarian assistance may have contradictory effects. UNRWA (the United Nations Relief and Works Agency for Palestine Refugees), created in 1949 to provide relief and development for more than 5 million Palestinian refugees after the 1948 and 1967 wars in the Middle East, fulfilled an important role in aiding Palestinian refugees. Nevertheless, there is also a strong argument that it has supported the Israeli occupation by helping to maintain the post-war status quo.

Since the end of the Cold War numerous forms of conflict resolution, citizen diplomacy, and informal forms of mediation have emerged as a result of civil society actors and capacities, often supported by international donors in places such as Cyprus, Sri Lanka, Israel/Palestine, and Northern Ireland. As a result, understandings of peace in policy and in practice have begun to include an everyday dimension of peace. This means that it is not enough to have a ceasefire or a peace treaty at the state level, but that society must also be safe to conduct everyday life. NGOs have become important actors in these processes, especially where they provide conflict resolution capacities, early warning of a possible impending conflict, and construct the institutions necessary for democratization and the rule of law to become integral to an emerging peace.

For example, two London-based organizations, Conciliation Resources and International Alert, work on the premise that the denial of human rights leads to conflict and they support local solutions to conflicts. The Carter Center, based in Atlanta, Georgia (USA), also operates on issues related to democratization, human rights, and conflict resolution. Organizations like International Crisis Group, based in Brussels, seek to report on, advocate, and draw attention to conflicts all over the world. Such organizations often draw on the funding of international donors and work closely with the UN, as well as with local NGOs, governments, and other actors in conflict and post-conflict zones around the world.

In addition, organizations such as UNESCO (United Nations Educational, Scientific and Cultural Organization) endeavour to connect international peace institutions to the civil peace. It has worked in a range of areas on developing a culture of peace, from education to gender and children's rights. This attempt to connect civil society and NGOs to international organizations aims to support a culture of peace across all levels.

At the end of the Cold War, a series of UN General Assembly resolutions called for humanitarian assistance to victims of emergencies and natural disasters, for access for accredited agencies, the establishment of relief corridors, and the establishment of the UN Department of Humanitarian Affairs to coordinate humanitarian intervention (though bound to the rules of sovereignty). Furthermore, during the Kurdish crisis in northern Iraq, UN Security Council Resolution 688 of 5 April 1991 facilitated humanitarian intervention involving a number of NGOs. In Bosnia, Security Council Resolution 771 of 13 August 1992 called for humanitarian organizations to have unimpeded access, but it became a point of controversy between the opposing sides in the war. However, during the collapse of the former Yugoslavia in the early 1990s, the international community found it very difficult to offer humanitarian assistance while the war was still in process. Similarly, in Somalia, after the collapse of the state in 1991, the UN was supposed to create conditions for the strengthening of civil society and offer humanitarian relief operations. The UN Secretary General's Special Representative attempted to bring in NGOs to facilitate this in order to involve local groups in the peace process. Similar patterns of subcontracting essential assistance for civil society were also tried in Haiti, Rwanda, and in Liberia, among many others during the 1990s, with varying degrees of success.

## Implications for the civil peace

The civil peace has had a significant impact on world affairs; it implies a more positive form of peace can be created, and also that different societies may have different aspirations or understandings of peace. It has driven the development of a range of rights and important UN conventions. These included among others the Declaration of Human Rights in 1948; the Convention on the Prevention and Punishment of the Crime of Genocide in 1948; the Convention on the Political Rights of Women in 1952; the Declaration on the Granting of Independence to Colonial Countries and Peoples in 1960; the International Covenant on Economic, Social, and Cultural Rights in 1966; the Declaration on the Right of Peoples to Peace in 1984; and the United Nations Declaration on the Rights of Indigenous Peoples in 2007. There have been many conventions, all aimed at producing a more positive form of peace in which institutions and states act in the interests of their citizens. They also point towards a hybrid form of peace.

The Millennium Assembly of the UN in 2000 and the Millennium Development Goals followed this logic. The UN agreed to focus on achieving the following goals by the year 2015: eradicating extreme poverty, achieving universal primary education, promoting gender equality and empowering women, reducing child mortality and improving maternal health, combating HIV/AIDS, malaria, and other diseases, and, finally, ensuring environmental sustainability and establishing a global partnership for development.

Not one of the targets set has so far been reached, but much progress has been made.

Many other non-governmentally influenced international campaigns have aimed to improve the lot of the peoples of the world. Such civil peace campaigns, in unison with international institutions, have highlighted the importance of avoiding the creation of dependency, being sensitive to the needs of local ownership, and being careful not to offend local or district officials and governments. They adhere to the injunction 'do no harm', often now written into the mandates of various international organizations.

Such dynamics mean that civil society actors are often described as 'norm entrepreneurs'. They privilege democracy, human rights, and forms of development in their micro-level interventions in society as well as in the realm of international relations. They contribute to a local, grassroots peace, based upon local community consent and legitimacy in the context of a global, transnational civil society of networks between civil society organizations. The work of OXFAM, Amnesty

International, Greenpeace, and many other groups concerned with issues like development and human rights, contributes to the civil peace.

Conversely, some commentators argue that NGOs and non-state actors are thinly veiled fronts for powerful state interests, in that they are dependent on state funding and so support state interests, particularly with respect to foreign policy, trade, and the extraction of primary resources such as oil. Donor states, agencies, and IFIs generally subcontract work to NGOs precisely because of their access to, and legitimacy within, civil society, and also because humanitarian, social, educational, conflict resolution, and developmental tasks play a significant role in the reconstruction of the state. Sometimes, however, it may be the case that organizations in civil society represent views and groupings opposed to peace, such as those resting on nationalist or sectarian identities or links, or engage in unequal and exploitative relationships with other socio-economic groups in society.

The development and mobilization of the civil peace and its civil society actors has helped alter the nature of the state from one that was often feudal or authoritarian to one that was more democratic, observing the rights of its diverse citizens, and also working for a modicum of equality between them. Many states, subject to civil and international pressure in the last century or more, eventually changed their focus from predatory behaviour at the expense of their own citizens, or territorial aggrandizement, to providing a degree of welfare and equality enshrined in law. This follows the old idea of a progressive, liberal social contract between citizen and state, but also indicates the citizen's capacity to campaign for change and reform at the international level.

These developments have enabled a re-envisioning of peace since the latter part of the 20th century, making a necessary contribution to the liberal peace. It depends on a range of processes in close association with major donor states (mainly northern states), international organizations like the UN, agencies like the United National Development Programme (UNDP) or United National High Commission for Refugees (UNHCR), or the World Bank. The World Bank, the Asian Development Bank, and the World Trade Organization, among many others, now encourage state relationships with civil society (even if some critics would argue that unmitigated capitalism undermines civil society at the same time). Overall, however, this has further enabled the civil peace to develop from the bottom up and from within society.

Recent human security approaches follow this logic. They involve a commitment to a just and sustainable settlement to conflict, the reframing of security debates to include human security, and the involvement of external non-state actors and indigenous non-state actors. This concept has been widely accepted in key policy circles and in global civil society's interconnected space that links civil society, NGOs, international agencies, and development donors.

# Chapter 8
# Peacekeeping, peacebuilding, and statebuilding

## Towards peacebuilding

As the liberal peace coalesced in modern international relations, there emerged four different generations of approaches for making peace, designed to consolidate the liberal peace system and international, state and civil architecture, which was by now widely accepted to be the most positive and sophisticated form of peace in history. By the latter part of the 20th century these had given birth to a range of processes designed to manage, resolve, or transform conflict:

(a) a first generation approach aimed at a negative peace, from the 1950s onwards (created during the 1956 Suez Crisis), in which neutral military intervention brought about ceasefires often through the UN;

(b) a second generation approach from the late 1960s more focused on social reconciliation and a positive peace;

(c) by the 1990s, a third generation of approaches focused on building liberal peace through development, peacekeeping, peacebuilding, statebuilding, democratization, creating a rule of law, promoting human rights, civil society, and capitalism. This also offered a positive form of peace, though a neoliberal variant of statebuilding which emerged in the early 2000s—as in Afghanistan—appeared to be happy with a negative peace;

(d)  a fourth generation approach, still developing, which combines
     the liberal peace with a recognition of local and contextual peace
     traditions. This may produce positive hybrid forms of peace, in
     which locally legitimacy and emancipatory goals combine with the
     liberal peace system. It follows a critical tradition aimed at social
     justice in everyday contexts, also anchored in an international
     architecture such as the UN system.

## Conflict management after World War II

The thinking that underlies the victor's peace has contributed to
modern 'conflict management' approaches in international
politics, which aimed at little more than maintaining a negative
peace. This represented a first generation of attempts to manage
international conflict and stabilize the international system.
Conflict management approaches developed after World War II.
They have sometimes included the use of force by coalitions of
states, but more often tools such as UN peacekeeping, high-level
diplomacy (meaning the involvement of senior politicians,
statesmen and women, and international bureaucrats like the UN
Secretary General) and the use of international mediation. Such
processes often produced 'zero-sum' outcomes in which a negative
peace consisted of unstable relations between 'winners' and 'losers'
in a conflict.

To this effect, the UN Charter stated:

> All Members shall settle their international disputes by peaceful
> means in such a manner that international peace and security, and
> justice, are not endangered.

> The parties to any dispute, the continuance of which is likely to
> endanger the maintenance of international peace and security,
> shall, first of all, seek a solution by negotiation, enquiry, mediation,
> conciliation, arbitration, judicial settlement, resort to regional
> agencies or arrangements, or other peaceful means of their own
> choice.

These binding statements are central to any modern conception of conflict management, aimed at maintaining international security. However, this type of security was envisaged in limited and state-centric, excluding non-state actors and non-state-centric, issues in conflict. The negative peace during much of the Cold War involved the preservation of the territorial integrity of states through conflict management approaches. The human rights of citizens were of secondary importance.

Reaching a ceasefire agreement, withdrawing foreign forces, establishing law and order, and achieving a comprehensive peace agreement at the diplomatic level were the key components of conflict management approaches. They aimed at supporting a basic minimum order without any overt violence. To achieve this any third parties involved in mediation or peacekeeping had to be neutral and impartial, or, alternatively, work according to their power and interests. International mediation as a diplomatic activity required interactions between states over territory, alliances, constitutional agreements, or boundaries, often led by a leader or by the UN. As mediation became more sophisticated, according to William Zartman (a professor of political science at Johns Hopkins University), it enabled the search for windows of opportunity provided by 'hurting stalemates' (where disputants are caught up in a painful situation where they could not win on the battlefield but neither could they afford to give up the struggle) and 'ripe moments' (where new opportunities arise for a settlement to occur). The disputants might be more likely to settle and mediators, diplomats, and peacekeeping operations would be able to mobilize.

Though not mentioned by name in the UN Charter, UN peacekeeping was probably the most innovative of modern conflict management approaches. Peacekeeping was developed by the UN Secretary General and his team in 1956 during the Suez Crisis in order to prevent it from sparking a major conflict between the superpowers. Since 1990, several generations of peacekeeping have spanned very limited operations that simply patrolled ceasefires to much more complex, multidimensional operations.

This early type of peacekeeping involved four main principles: that the force should be defensive rather than offensive; that it should not include troops drawn from major powers (to enhance its neutrality); that it should be impartial; and that it should have consent and not intervene in the dispute. In this way a small and symbolic force, cheaply run, could offer symbolic support for peace and security, help uphold the UN Charter, and not take great risks because it had the consent of the parties to the dispute, whether the superpowers in the UN Security Council or armies and guerrilla fighters on the ground. It could also provide a calmer environment in which peace talks might be held.

The earliest forms of modern peacekeeping were essentially observer missions or disengagement missions (as in the missions in Kashmir (1947) or the Middle East (1948) in the 1950s), but they quickly developed into forms intended to provide the conditions of stability in which diplomacy, mediation, and negotiation could begin alongside peacekeeping forces (as in Cyprus from 1964 onwards). Many of the peacekeeping missions since 1956, and the Suez Crisis (1956–7), aimed at facilitating independence of colonial territories and enabling colonial powers to withdraw while saving face. They were aimed at preventing small wars, as in Cyprus in 1963 or 1974, from escalating into major conflicts. They normally patrolled agreed ceasefires, and tried to oversee the withdrawal of troops and the creation of a peace agreement, as after the Suez Crisis in 1956 or in Cyprus from 1964. In other words they tried to support a negative peace that would last only for as long as the peacekeepers were present.

After the end of the Cold War many conflicts flared up, in the Balkans, Africa, Central America, and Africa. UN peacekeeping again endeavoured to implement the terms of prior peace agreements negotiated by the UN Secretary General or other international mediators in places such as Namibia (1989–90), where an agreement between South Africa and local leaders led to Namibian Independence overseen by the UN. There were also similar UN forces sent around this time to implement agreements which brought civil wars to an end in Angola and Mozambique. Observer missions also monitored the transition into peace after the end of civil wars in Nicaragua and El Salvador.

More ambitious missions also occurred, as in Cambodia where the UN also acted as a transitional government during the process of building a democracy (1992–3). They became more involved in building a liberal and, therefore, positive form of peace. By the late 1990s and under increasing pressure, the UN was trying to conduct peacekeeping without local consent, as in Bosnia-Herzegovina, exposing peacekeepers and international staff to the risk of being drawn into the conflict rather than being perceived as neutral third parties.

The evolution of peacekeeping occurred because the practice of conflict management in places like DR Congo or Cyprus in the early 1960s had failed to cope with the weaknesses of a negative peace or respond to local demands for a positive peace. Early forms of peacekeeping achieved some mitigation of open violence but rarely a comprehensive peace settlement (perhaps with the exception of the Camp David Accords between Israel and Egypt after wars in 1967 and 1973, though this was mediated with some persuasiveness by US President Carter in 1978). Negative peace suffers from the same weakness as the victor's peace: it needs permanent military and material guarantees, otherwise any peace process it engenders may collapse.

## Peace through conflict resolution

A second generation attempt to address the underlying dynamics of conflict, and to resolve and reconcile conflicting parties, focused on the rights and needs of citizens rather than states. This was partly in reaction to the limited goals of the previous approach.

It aimed at creating a 'win–win' outcome (where all parties feel they have won as a result of the peace process) driven by the needs of civil society in particular. It focused on the root causes of conflict from the perspective of individuals, groups, and societies, and on mutual accommodation at this level of analysis (it is often described as 'track II', track I being formal diplomacy, mediation, and negotiation). From this perspective, conflict arises out of a repression of basic human needs and is a social as well as a psychological phenomenon. Human needs are now often viewed as universal and non-negotiable in the UN and donor system. Second generation approaches saw injustice as a source of social unrest and human needs offered a framework for understanding about the causes of conflict, how it might be resolved, and how reconciliation and justice could be achieved, rather than merely managing enmity. This civil society-oriented discourse aimed to construct a positive peace addressing the societal roots of conflict and discriminatory and inequitable social, economic, and political structures.

Second generation approaches highlight human security rather than state security. From this theoretical basis a number of new methods for peacemaking emerged. Citizen diplomacy, conflict resolution, and similar approaches became common around the world in places such as Cyprus, the Middle East, Northern Ireland, or Sri Lanka as an alternative and innovative way to reconcile societies. In these cases, in the 1990s and early 2000s, informal 'back channels' were created between a range of political and informal civil society actors across conflict lines. Meetings often took place informally between social groups to discuss local matters and how to improve everyday life, as well as to discuss broader visions of a peace process. International mediators found ways of promoting these and avoiding the usual obstacles relating to status and power emerging. In all of these cases informal channels of communication facilitated a peace process that eventually had a major impact on the official level and improved security significantly, at least for a time.

This second generation approach was particularly successful in Northern Ireland when the peace process began after 1994. The peace process in Northern Ireland took place at the elite and the social level, and was cemented by massive civil society and economic investment from the British government and the EU to iron out structural and economic inequalities between its communities. There was also a parallel agreement between the main governments historically involved and the creation of new and improved political institutions (the Good Friday Agreement of 1998). However, the potential of these processes in other locations such as Israel/Palestine and Sri Lanka was not realized despite very promising starts in the 1990s. Their peace processes reverted to nationalistic, power-driven, formal processes, and eventually were not able to overcome the usual problems associated with sovereignty, militarization, and the inherent bias of pre-existing institutions. Conflict resolution approaches have, however, made it clear that in any society a peace process should meet political, social, and economic needs and rights.

## Conflict transformation, peacebuilding, and statebuilding

In the last twenty years a very significant and innovative international peace architecture has developed. This is a third generation approach to both ending conflict and constructing a more advanced form of peace. It has involved large-scale and external forms of intervention since the early 1990s, from countries like Cambodia, Bosnia, Sierra Leone, Timor Leste, Afghanistan, and many others.

This approach has been influenced by conflict transformation theory, which argues that what is necessary to make peace is a process that transforms the relationships, interests, nature of state and society which feeds a conflict. This is a long-term and multidimensional process, aimed at addressing the roots of conflict, including perceptions, communications, inequality, and social injustice. Liberal peacebuilding is heavily indebted to such approaches.

There are varying estimates, but by 2008 about 110,000 personnel were deployed in conflict or post-conflict countries populated by a total of 100 million people. These operations include a range of components, such as military intervention, democratization, and development, managed by international organizations such as the UN and the World Bank, foreign donors, and many regional and international agencies. They aimed to build a positive peace and focused on security, democracy, human rights, the rule of law, development, free trade, and a vibrant civil society. In the last twenty or so years liberal peacebuilding and statebuilding have become the dominant approaches for responding to localized and regional conflicts.

## Liberal peacebuilding

Once the liberal peace had been widely agreed by the international community in the early 1990s, the next step for the international community was to devise ways of installing it in conflict environments. As earlier chapters have outlined, liberal peacebuilding links peace and security directly with development, democracy, the rule of law, human rights, and a vibrant civil society in a modern state framework. This is embedded in a system of global governance, international law, and trade.

This top–down architecture only offers part of the picture, however. Peacebuilding was initially theorized in the peace research literature as a grassroots, bottom–up process in which a local consensus within society led to a positive peace. As the concept evolved, it came to represent a convergence with the agendas of human rights, development, democratization, and human security, and in practice it also had to bring together conflicting interests of major states in the UN Security Council. A convergence of international norms and interests—a peacebuilding consensus—culminated in the contemporary liberal peacebuilding project. After the end of the Cold War this was in part based upon the development of more ambitious and integrated forms of peacekeeping, which evolved rapidly from multidimensional forms at first with the consent of local actors and in a multilateral form, and then, on occasion, without their consent. As a result, the demands on the role of the UN and its supporting actors multiplied and diversified enormously in terms of the tasks they undertook to build peace and the many locations around the world where they did so.

A number of UN documents starting with *An Agenda for Peace* in 1992 described peacebuilding in detail. This UN document, akin to a Cold War peace settlement, described peacebuilding as 'action to identify and support structures which will tend to strengthen and solidify peace in order to avoid a relapse into conflict'. In 2007 the UN Secretary General provided a comprehensive definition:

> Peacebuilding involves a range of measures targeted to reduce the risk of lapsing or relapsing into conflict by strengthening national capacities at all levels for conflict management, and to lay the foundations for sustainable peace and development. Peacebuilding strategies must be coherent and tailored to specific needs of the country concerned, based on national ownership, and should comprise a carefully prioritized, sequenced, and therefore relatively narrow set of activities aimed at achieving the above objectives.

However, this approach is constrained by the need to consider sovereign states and their right of non-intervention, as well as its implicit claim that peace should be built according to a universal formula, repeated throughout most contemporary policy documentation on peacebuilding.

A related evolution occurred with the concept of security in the UN and in the emerging 'peace industry'. At least until the end of the Cold War security mainly revolved around whether wars were fought between states, and whether a state's territory was secure. This was regardless of what was happening inside the state, which was often a site for authoritarian or totalitarian rule: often there was ongoing oppression of specific identity or socio-economic groups by the dominant elite. By the mid-1990s, as previously noted, many of the world's policymakers began to think in terms of human security, reviving US President Roosevelt's old post-World War II slogan, 'freedom from fear, freedom from want'.

Since the early 1990s UN Integrated Missions endeavoured to support the broad ambitions of peacebuilding, as in the Balkans in the early 1990s along with other actors (such as NATO, the EU, and the OSCE). The early post-Cold War peacekeeping operations in Namibia, Cambodia, Angola, Mozambique, and El Salvador seemed to offer the hope that the peace engendered by UN intervention could go beyond patrolling ceasefires and would instead contribute to the democratization and liberal reform of failing and failed states. This blueprint was also used in Cambodia, Bosnia, Kosovo, Sierra Leone, Liberia, DR Congo, and East Timor and others during the 1990s and 2000s. Liberal peacebuilding came to represent a multilevel approach, attempting to address the local, state, and regional aspects of, and actors in, conflict. It has become multidimensional in nature in that it brings together a wide range of actors who were able to deal with a wide range of issues and dynamics.

So far, the record of peacebuilding has been mixed. Many operations in different locations have merely resulted in rather authoritarian regimes so far. This is because the process is inconsistent in its design, or is inefficient and ill coordinated by international actors, or because deficiencies have arisen because local actors are given too much say and thus insert their illiberalism, nationalism, and interests into the process.

To avoid such tendencies, international administration of post-conflict environments (meaning that the UN or specific groups of states assume responsibility for another state emerging from conflict) became more common again. This approach was used in Bosnia-Herzegovina, and Kosovo, Timor Leste, and to some degree in Afghanistan. However, in Afghanistan and Iraq in the 2000s, more interventionary approaches were used. These aimed at producing regional and international stability while reforming the state (a process often now called 'statebuilding'). They have been widely regarded as only achieving a negative peace.

Peacebuilding approaches draw upon the idea that peace can be built by external actors such as the UN, donors, NGOs, and foreign militaries, based on liberal norms to create a liberal state. By the start of the 21st century, an even more ambitious agenda emerged via the *Millennium Development Goals* (2000), and a new doctrine called the *Responsibility to Protect* (2005). This implied that sovereignty entailed responsibility to citizens, and if a state undermined the human rights of its citizens, committed acts of genocide, war crimes, crimes against humanity, and ethnic cleansing, the international community might intervene.

The international community, led by the UN and key donors, designed these policies to achieve economic stability, prosperity, and to guarantee human rights as well as the rule of law. They were in part driven by the demands made by electorates in many developed states in order to support populations in local contexts who bore the brunt of conflict. Such approaches have also been resisted by some states (such as Russia and China, among others) which argue that such trends are little better than new forms of colonialism, representing northern/Western hegemony, and that they are an attack on their sovereign rights.

Even so, peacebuilding processes now involve tens of thousands of military and civilian personnel working in post-conflict locations across the world. In sum liberal peacebuilding continued the shift towards a much more positive understanding of peace. Through the adoption of liberal norms and institutions, as well as neoliberal forms of development, encapsulated within a modern state framework, liberal peacebuilding offered a broader view of peace. It also offered what appeared to be a globally applicable blueprint method, to which end the UN Peacebuilding Commission was established in 2005. Working in countries such as Burundi, Sierra Leone, Guinea Bissau, and Central African Republic, the UN Peacebuilding Commission, Peacebuilding Fund, and Peacebuilding Support Office are involved in integrating and coordinating the range of processes that occur.

Yet, liberal peacebuilding has also been widely criticized for being illiberal (resting on military intervention), inefficient, and ill coordinated, for assuming that promoting democracy, human rights, and trade are enough to make peace, and for not paying enough attention to local preferences and needs. On average, at least two out of five peace settlements during this period have collapsed within a few years, though improvements in peace and security around the world have been achieved in the last twenty-five years.

## Statebuilding

In the early 2000s, a new doctrine called statebuilding emerged, which represented a significant retreat from the normative aspirations of the liberal peace (relating to human rights in particular). Increasing state weakness, in the areas of security, crime, terrorism, as well as deviations from the liberal norms of the developed north, were seen as threats to international peace and security. Many of the world's leaders thought that this was the lesson of the 2000s, especially in relation to states like Afghanistan, Somalia, North Korea, Pakistan, and others. Such failing and post-conflict states were a threat to the international system, becoming breeding grounds for a dangerous mix of terrorism, poverty, crime, trafficking, and humanitarian catastrophe, which might have spilt over into other states.

The aim of statebuilding is to create prosperous and stable liberal states framed by a 'good governance' agenda, via externalized strategies of intervention. With the apparent limitations of peacebuilding especially in terms of its susceptibility to mission creep (as in Somalia, Bosnia-Herzegovina, and Kosovo in the 1990s, where international actors became part of the conflicts) statebuilding appeared to offer a unified theory designed to produce an intervention with a small or 'light footprint'—as in Afghanistan. It implied that any international intervention would not turn into a far-reaching form of trusteeship. This, it was calculated, would be less objectionable to international or local partners than a major intervention.

States that emerge from statebuilding should provide their citizens with security, goods, services, law, and institutions. This may also facilitate democracy, rights, transitional and long-term justice, integration, and a rule of law, provide for basic needs, and mitigate identity conflicts. According to the 1997 World Bank report, 'The State in a Changing World', this type of state framework has a set of core functions, ranging from the minimalist functions of security, law, and order, to the 'activist' functions associated with legitimate institutions, public services, welfare, and social support.

Statebuilding is assumed to capture both local and international forms of legitimacy and especially the local desire for sovereignty. It converts these into a political architecture with territorial control, political stability, and economic viability. It offers a process of modernization whereby previous institutions are brought into line with the current models associated with international expectations. Its genealogy reaches back to the reconstruction and nation-building experiments after the US civil war, in Germany and Japan, and much of Western Europe after World War II.

This understanding of the state anticipates a range of core functions that provides security and consolidates democracy, rights, and prosperity. The state is responsible for security and justice, revenue creation and collection, providing basic services, and creating jobs, and the better the state is at these tasks the more legitimacy it would receive from its citizens. The state focuses on security, law, and property rights, and protects the marginalized. It should be decentralized, competitive, and meritocratic. Statebuilding itself emanates from international organizations, institutions, and donors, their norms and political and economic practices, passed down through systems of global governance, international conventions, regional organizations, to the state and its citizens.

The statebuilding project has suffered from the same flaws as liberal peacebuilding: a lack of a peace dividend and a failure to offer security, an everyday peace or social justice, as graphically illustrated in contemporary Afghanistan.

## Assessing recent achievements

Liberal peacebuilding and statebuilding represent the most advanced Western and global consensus on the importance of international institutions and open markets, and on democracy and human rights, in preventing conflict as well as attending to its underlying causes. This consensus also includes a broad range of non-Western states (though non-developed and subaltern actors are less represented). It has had some success in reducing violence and inducing some compliance with liberal norms, institutions, law, and markets. Yet there have been few outright 'successes' to speak of. Of course, this depends how success is defined. If it depends on a state not relapsing into violence, available data shows that about half of post-war environments in which the UN has worked achieve a negative peace at least for the first five years after the end of the conflict. The number of interstate and civil wars have been reduced as have the number of deaths. The numbers of durable and negotiated settlements also appear to have increased. Thus, this is at least a basis for a more positive peace to emerge.

However, out of 18 or more UN attempts at democratization since the end of the Cold War, 13 had suffered some form of authoritarian regime within several years. In addition, the international financial institutions like the World Bank have used structural adjustment and development projects that have failed to provide the sorts of economic opportunities and welfare that would be expected to provide a quick 'peace dividend'. The relationship between peacebuilding and justice has also been controversial. Justice has often remained subservient to stability because some influential individuals and organizations in conflict environments are implicated in violence, corruption, or crimes against humanity. In effect, liberal peacebuilding and statebuilding has become a system of governance in post-conflict and development settings rather than a process of reconciliation.

What this indicates is a failure to achieve goals of peacebuilding and statebuilding, or to come to terms with the lived experiences of individuals and their needs in everyday life, or vis-à-vis their culture and traditions. There have been several common complaints:

(i)   that there are not enough resources available for the vast scale of making peace;
(ii)  that there is a lack of local capacity, skill, participation, or consent;
(iii) that there is a lack of coordination and too much duplication amongst the international actors;
(iv)  that the process is mainly owned by international actors rather than by its recipients;

(v)  that the issues that face society in social and welfare terms are ignored;

(vi)  that peacebuilding and statebuilding is mainly driven by neoliberal marketization and development agendas rather than reconciliation;

(vii)  that it perpetuates local and international inequality and elite predation.

The liberal peace framework has aimed to reform or create neoliberal democracies open for international trade rather than social democracies to support their citizens' welfare. This is despite the huge volume of evidence about the importance of poverty and inequality in maintaining conflict and its many stratifications. Peaceful societies are generally more equal, as are peaceful regions.

Privately, many policymakers and bureaucrats agree with this idea, and the UN, World Bank, and many donors and NGOs have constantly adjusted their approaches to engage with such problems. Current discussions of 'local ownership' and 'participation' for example in the UN and World Bank are indicative of concern that peacebuilding and statebuilding are more or less irrelevant to some or many post-conflict citizens' everyday lives.

What have instead emerged are fragile states propped up by international actors, from the UN, the World Bank, to national donors or international NGOs. However, much has been learned about peacebuilding through such experiences, including the need for local power systems, political and economic frameworks, society, religion, and culture to be part of any framework for peace. Liberal peace is now being supplanted by hybrid or post-liberal forms of peace, which draw on liberal peacebuilding and local context factors simultaneously. This is significant because peacebuilding and statebuilding are mainly being applied outside of the Western or northern contexts where they were initially developed.

# Chapter 9
# Hybrid forms of peace

In a step beyond liberal peace frameworks, hybrid forms of peace are emerging in diverse locations around the world. Local patterns of politics based on contextual social, cultural, and historical norms, identities, and material resources influence hybrid peace along with western/northern peace thinking related to democracy, rule of law, human rights, and a vibrant civil society. What is emerging is neither strictly a liberal nor a local form of peace, but a hybrid, formed through political contestation involving a range of actors, their preferences, and security interests. In some cases, a negative hybrid peace may be emerging, as in Afghanistan where warlords and external peacebuilders make very uncomfortable company, but in others there is the possibility of more positive hybrid forms, as in Timor Leste or Sierra Leone, where local customary law and governance may be slowly aligning with the modern state.

Such processes have significant implications for any emancipatory form of peace. It should reflect the interests, identities, and needs of all actors, state and non-state. It would aim at mutual accommodation across identity groups and regions of the world, as well as autonomy and social justice. An everyday form of peace is its objective as well as complementing the liberal peace that emerged from the internationalist dreams of the 20th century. It raises the question—in an era when the West is no longer internationally dominant—of how local forms of legitimacy, or alternative political, social, and economic systems, and norms of peace can engage with international forms. Can international understandings of a liberal human rights regime (part of the civil peace and crucial to a liberal social contract) be reconciled with local, customary, or religious practices in very diverse locations around the world? A hybrid form of peace may therefore transcend the third generation peacebuilding and statebuilding approaches. A fourth generation approach may include more localized and contextual traditions and approaches rooted in each post-conflict society. It would also have to deal with the very significant global inequalities that remain between states and societies around the world. A hybrid peace may represent an evolution beyond a positive peace.

## Hybrid forms of peace: a fourth generation of peace?

In Somalia, despite the collapsed nature of the state, many local communities have organized themselves to maintain stability, justice, and the economy through customary and ad hoc informal institutions, as notably in Puntland and Somaliland. In Cambodia a relatively authoritarian democracy has emerged since the early 1990s' peacebuilding, where a vibrant civil society, particularly in the realms of human rights, has kept pressure on the government. In Bosnia-Herzegovina, the conditions of a weak, post-war state have been partially alleviated by both international support and local communities' attempts at mitigating them. In Timor Leste, as in Liberia, Mozambique, Sierra Leone, Guatemala, the Solomon Islands, and many others, international and local cooperation has produced a specifically contextual version of peace, to varying degrees incorporating customary practices. Local organizations, operating in civil society, often informally, and combining local customs and justice with the emerging modern state, have been vital to this process. The state has often been reshaped by these processes, though its elites may also resist the required reforms and compromises. It may require, as in Afghanistan, difficult compromises with tribal groups and their historical practices, including the Taliban and various warlords, which would certainly involve significant reform on their behalf. Thousands of internationally supported local development committees and NGOs have been essential to this process and for creating wider stability.

In general, these examples indicate a slow movement towards what might be called *a post-liberal peace*, one where international norms and institutions interact with different, contextual, and localized polities. This process capitalizes on the core of the original conflict resolution and peacebuilding agendas. It addresses human needs and root causes, connecting the new state or polity with older, locally recognizably legitimate agendas and engages with grassroots and the most marginalized members of post-conflict polities.

Along these lines it has become accepted that national ownership and contextual specificity are necessary for peacebuilding. Basic security, a rule of law, political institutions and processes, basic services including health and education, core functions of government, and employment remain part of this new phase of peacebuilding. Employment generation, economic vitalization, and transitional safety nets are seen as a way of distributing a peace dividend.

Further attempts to refine international policies have followed this line of thought, notably the World Bank 'World Development Report 2011', which talks of a 'social compact', the Busan Partnership Agreement on development cooperation and a 'New Deal for Engagement in Fragile States' in late 2001, and the 2012 UNDP report 'Governance for Peace: Securing the Social Contract'. These documents illustrate an evolution in policymaking that reflects an attempt to develop a fourth generation approach. They mention the social compact, the need for legitimacy, people's security, justice (but not social justice), economic development, and 'fair services'. Transnational global civil society has yet again been instrumental in pushing for this 'new deal'.

## Local contributions to peace

This understanding of the potential of peacebuilding in a more contextual sense has long been present in post-conflict sites, where local groups have often formed to bring about peace for themselves on a small but effective and now widely replicated scale.

For example, in the 1990s conflict resolution workshops run in Cyprus by mainly American or European scholars allowed people interested in peace to meet across the green line, which had divided Greek and Turkish Cypriots since 1974 or even earlier. They valued the contact with their 'enemies' and the ability to debate, but they also felt that the conduct of the workshops glossed over the difficult political, economic, identity, and justice issues they faced. On the other hand, the academics that ran them were often frustrated by what they saw as local tendencies not to cooperate, to remain dogmatic, not to engage in the way they wanted, and yet to appear to be dependent on them for any contact with the other side.

Despite all of these problems, local participants were able to use the process to build a peace constituency, which did not represent a single consensus about a peace settlement for the island, but allowed a sophisticated form of peaceful coexistence to emerge amongst the members of these 'inter-communal groups'. In the latest formal attempts to develop a peace process even the island's two governments and political leaders recognized the importance of such civil society movements, after years of ignoring their potential.

In Mozambique and Namibia, since the end of their conflicts in the 1990s, government or internationals have not addressed social and economic issues fully, given the history of colonization and white settlement. Civil society is often described as weak or absent, dependent upon fickle donor priorities and funds. Nevertheless, local organizations have continued to engage in human rights, development, education, or training work, often within a subsistence context (meaning they do not receive any donor or international support). When such organizations decide to work in this manner, without significant donor support, they often find that they are able to survive and develop their own approaches. In Mozambique, one NGO is using traditional musical instruments in rural areas to teach people about pluralism, peace, and coexistence. Another organization has developed its own small arms decommissioning project, which has earned worldwide fame. Weapons are turned into sculptures and pieces of art. Such small activities often have a broader social significance even if political and economic obstacles to peace remain. Their ambitions are captured in a famous sculpture outside the UN Building in New York (see Figure 7).

In Guatemala, a prosperous European settler community has dominated politics and the economy before and even since the peace process of the 1990s. The majority community of Mayan people, often living in rural settings in relative poverty, barely even recognize that they live in the same state. They have developed numerous ways of preserving their culture and identity and have increasingly become more successful in finding spaces in which they can survive and coexist with the modern state. They have worked hard to have their culture and cosmology included in national and international fora, and so are carving out hybrid peace.

In Sri Lanka, despite very difficult circumstances for any peace process during the 2000s, certain local organizations have navigated around the constraints imposed by separatist violence, nationalist and elitist government, and ethnic and religious chauvinism, with skill that other internationals, such as mediators

7. Non-Violence—The Knotted Gun (1980) is a bronze sculpture by Swedish artist Carl Fredrik Reuterswärd which is placed outside the UN Building in New York

from countries like Norway, foreign donors, or the UN, have not been able to emulate. While the latter have been undermined by rapacious and paranoid local politics, local organizations (which in the interests of their safety should not be named), working in the areas of human rights and peacebuilding, have managed to maintain their roles of advocacy and accountability despite difficult, changing local conditions. They have managed with a mixture of international support and their own capacity and knowledge to offer the possibility of a hybrid peace.

In both Kosovo and Bosnia-Herzegovina after the wars and during the late 1990s and early 2000s, international actors became frustrated with their local counterparts' tendencies to obstruct or 'go slow' on institutional reforms designed to bring the liberal state into being, particularly where these demanded social, cultural, economic, reform, or identity changes. The result in Bosnia was deadlock over the reform of the state while in Kosovo it brought into being a contested state. In Bosnia local non-cooperation at the elite political level with the various international actors made developing the liberal peace very difficult in a highly fragmented state. In response, a number of civil society organizations on the ground, involved in human rights and transitional justice matters, and cultural projects, emerged in an attempt to speed up progress in resolving the country's various problems (though not necessarily conforming to international expectations of a liberal peace). In Kosovo, a range of organizations had undertaken to provide many of the services that the state had refused them during the 1980s, and after the war in 1999, they emerged from the shadows to become part of the new state. Both phenomena denote a potential hybrid form of peace and state emerging.

In Timor Leste since independence in 2002 and during the UN peacekeeping operation and especially after the recurrence of violence in 2006, local actors have been crucial in building a hybrid peace that has both social and political dimensions. Two of the most visible examples were the return to the landscape of 'sacred houses' and the creation of a social welfare system. Sacred houses are centres of family and social life, where local politics, arrangements, and economic support are decided, and where celebrations and ceremonies take place that bind communities, including conflict resolution ceremonies (see Figure 8). Their re-emergence is indicative of a deeper stabilization where international approaches had failed. Income from the Timor Gap oil and gas reserves, combined with a sense at the highest levels in government that a peace dividend needed to be distributed more directly by the state, and that the state had to reflect Timorese identity and history more closely, has more recently made peacebuilding more relevant to people's daily lives. As a result Timor Leste has become more stable and, of course, hybrid.

In the Solomon Islands, there are similar dynamics emerging in the post-conflict period. Most communities gain their law and justice, representation, and welfare from localized, customary, or

8. These buildings are known as *uma lulik* or sacred houses in Timor Leste

church-oriented institutions and processes. The modern state appears to them to be distant and often predatory, as do international markets. The Ministry for National Unity, Reconciliation, and Peace, established in 2009, has a very clear understanding of the contextual difficulties that the liberal peace system finds itself in, as well as an understanding of how local institutions, along with the liberal peace system, may offer empowerment and an alternative. This includes incorporating the customary system of elders and chiefs, customary law, the role of the churches, and the imagining of some specific cultural and historical symbols and identity formations that make the state relevant to its people. As in Timor Leste, a parallel form of politics to the modern peacebuilding process exists that internationals can barely comprehend. In Timor Leste, the modern state seems to be beginning to converge with these. This has yet to happen in the Solomon Islands in a formal sense, but informally, it is beginning. For example, a team of local and international constitutional lawyers are now working on the implications of a merger of state and customary institutions, a process that has also begun across the region.

This is also something that Afghanistan's President Hamid Karzai has called for in the context of Afghanistan. He developed his 'big tent' strategy to try to be inclusive of difficult actors such as the Taliban and a range of factions. However, this attempt at creating a state inclusive of powerful actors has led to its co-option by warlords and a continuing Taliban rebellion, underlining the weaknesses of statebuilding as an elite practice that is supposed to trickle down. However, Karzai argues that liberal democracy can be achieved but only if it respects local identity, religion, tradition, and society.

Encouragingly for liberal peacebuilding's supporters, local agents of peacebuilding often seek to develop relations with international donors. They draw on arguments in favour of democracy, human rights, free markets, and a rule of law, but also want to localize these. This requires exceptions and modifications to account for local contextual dynamics, sometimes confronting liberal norms, sometimes learning from them.

What is notable about most peacebuilding and statebuilding cases is that inequality and social exclusion (i.e. very high statistical indicators of poverty and inequality) are often little changed from the point at which a peace process began. This means that there has not been much of a peace dividend in everyday life in practice (though there has been a security dividend).

International assistance and enablement are necessary for peace to emerge in many of these locations, but ultimately emerging post-liberal and hybrid forms of peace depend on 'local ownership' to attain local legitimacy.

## Peace formation

The difficulties faced by peacebuilding and statebuilding policy raise the question of how contributions to peace from a range of informal local actors may be understood and externally supported. Collaboration and cooperation has been a key motivating factor for the formation of society and polities throughout human history in villages, communities, cities, states, and international organizations. It is widely accepted by anthropologists that peace systems emerge side by side with violence and war. Trust networks, civil society, and social movements mobilize over issues pertaining to violence and inequality, which interfere with peace and order. In other words, at least partly, a society desires to be peaceful, orients its cultural framework in that direction, and produces the social, political, economic, and institutional means to do so.

There are a range of potential spaces in which 'peace formation' processes may arise. Peace formation may draw on social, kin, and customary networks. It may include many different types of association, from unions to charities or regional trade networks. It may require formal international support for civil society. A rich web of relationships and networks is emerging from the local to the global that oppose embedded injustices and inequalities. The capacity for self-organization for non-violent resistance or to provide support, public services, and even security and policing, where the state is non-existent or incapable, has been a common occurrence, as the case of Somalia has illustrated since the early 1990s. It is often aimed at providing public services—health, education, and basic security and needs—in an everyday setting.

Basing peace projects on locally legitimate institutions, processes, customs, identities, and actors and their needs is vital. Any such process will inevitably be a political choice, probably best made by a wide range of actors on the ground and enabled internationally. These processes blur the lines between formal and informal dynamics, the state, custom, and the traditional. Often women's groups are at the forefront, from Liberia to Bangladesh and Brazil. It places society, the village, the community, and the city at the centre of peace, rather than the state, security, and markets.

This deeper fabric of peace agency in local contexts, even if heavily disrupted by conflict, tends to have pre-existed most state and international level interventions. Conflict and the many interventions that occur during a peace process may also spur innovation and new social and political projects to emerge which help transform the conflict into a new political agreement. It may utilize new forms of media and communications, not to mention transport and trade connections, or informal networks through academic or global social movements or INGOs.

Without external support, of course, what such local mobilization can achieve in terms of peace formation may be very limited. Likewise, without local peace formation dynamics, international actors will probably be ineffective in promoting change or transformation, resulting in at best a negative hybrid form of peace. Peace formation dynamics contribute to the nature of the state and, to some degree, the shape of the international system, offering the possibility of a locally and internationally legitimate positive hybrid peace.

There were hints of peace formation in early post-Cold War peacebuilding frameworks. In post-war El Salvador UNESCO supported a Programme on 'Establishing a Culture of Peace' in 1992 that recognized that human development, poverty reduction, and addressing root causes also meant engaging with peace in cultural terms. By 1995, programmes were under way in Mozambique, Burundi, and the Philippines among other countries, to connect peacemaking with social values, assumptions, and historical perspectives and structures, eventually becoming part of a national culture. This approach was aimed at respect for difference, solidarity, and social justice in general, and the establishment of a wide range of venues and spaces of dialogue in which rights, representation, and justice might emerge. They would eventually coalesce into institutions, it was hoped. Local peace architectures link grassroots organizations, local peace councils and committees, with local and national governmental institutions.

After the Lome Peace Accord in Sierra Leone in 1999, a Commission for the Consolidation of Peace was established along with national Commissions for Democracy, Human Rights, and others. The UN Peacebuilding Commission also helped to coordinate these. A parliamentary group also containing civil society members was established to work on a 'national peace infrastructure', which has included a range of fora, including a women's forum. Similarly, in Timor Leste UNDP has supported a Ministry of Peacebuilding's engagement with land and gender issues. Local peace councils of elders and activists have to become integrated into formal decentralized government as well as a National Peace Council, aimed at mediating conflict using local tools. Gradually the local structure has built up into a national structure, with varying degrees of success. Nepal also has a Ministry of Peace and Reconstruction along similar lines. South Sudan has established a Ministry for Peace aimed at a comprehensive implementation of the 2005 peace agreement, as well as using traditional methods, aimed at increasing the breadth of stakeholders in a peace process, improving the participation of civil society and communities, and enabling a broad reconciliation.

To some extent peace formation and its translation into peace infrastructures draws on local and historic practices of conflict management and resolution. In Somaliland in the early 1990s, localized peace agreements led by local elders utilizing customary law eventually resulted in a constitutional structure that included elected party representatives as well as a clan-oriented upper house. This grew out of widespread but localized peace conferences and discussions across Somaliland driven by the grassroots as well as business, clan, and political leaders, which has resulted in a reasonably stable polity, though it is as yet unrecognized as a state.

In Afghanistan, there are long-standing traditions of conflict resolution by tribal elders, village councils, the *jirga* dialogues, and the *Peace Shuras* or *Councils*, at local, district, and national level. These have become part of a more formal understanding of peace and stabilization, through the Community Development Councils and the National Solidarity Programme run by a government ministry, which, though far from successful, have become part of the international expectation about the nature of the state that will emerge.

In Kenya after the post-election violence of 2007, an Open Forum was created and a *Citizen's Agenda for Peace* was developed. Individuals gathered from all sectors of society in the weeks immediately after the conflict broke out. This was based on a peace movement started previously by a group of women in 1993, which led to the formation of a series of peace committees.

A National Policy on Peacebuilding and Conflict Management emerged in 2009, and peace committees in all districts were set up according to the National Accord and Reconciliation Act of 2008. This process drew in a number of ministries and levels of government and the media, and was also connected to the high-level peace process. Crucially, it was driven and legitimized by civil society and at the grassroots.

Such agendas influenced the 2011 Busan Agreement on a 'New Deal for Engagement in Fragile States' amongst the main international donors. This referred to core peacebuilding and statebuilding goals, and emphasized the need for legitimate politics, people's security, and justice, drawing on the Millennium Development Goals. The G7+ (an organization of so-called 'fragile states'—the 'club that everyone wants to leave'—including Timor Leste, Somalia, Sierra Leone, and fifteen others) influenced this agreement. Such developments have brought to the fore the notion that societies build peace and states, not only donors or state elites. This has meant 'putting the last first': a partial reversal, and has certainly led to a refinement of Western knowledge about peace.

# Epilogue: new agendas for peace

> ...the Culture of Peace is a set of values, attitudes, modes of
> behaviour and ways of life that reject violence and prevent
> conflicts by tackling their root causes to solve problems
> through dialogue and negotiation among individuals,
> groups, and nations.
>
> UN Resolution A/Res/52/13, 20 November 1997
> and A/Res/53/243, 6 October 1999

## New agendas for peace

The older notions of peace that were the subject of the first
two-thirds of this introduction have become less relevant to the
modern world. Peacemaking and the complex machinery it
requires has advanced considerably throughout history. When
confronted with transnational problems and political tensions
which relate to inequality, environmental unsustainability,
unstable flows of global capital, the arms trade, human trafficking,
and nuclear proliferation, new agendas for, and new forms of,
peace are clearly required.

The last few decades have illustrated both the potential and the
weaknesses of these methods. New forms are complex and would
need to sustain everyday life commensurate with local-level
socio-historical norms, institutions, and law, as well as a state and

international architecture of peace. The international community would be broadly attuned to support local everyday patterns of peace. This will probably not lead to a world government (to the disappointment of some liberal internationalists, and the relief of others attuned to political and identity differences), however, but instead may form a world community, made up of interlocking 'peaces'. It may include different types of states, institutions, and norms, in the light of the long-standing truism that only cooperation, inclusivity, and redistribution can maintain an ever-evolving peace infrastructure. History illustrates that this is an inescapable fact of human existence.

The UNESCO definition of a 'culture of peace' cited above represents one of the most sophisticated institutional understandings so far. Yet, as the World Bank estimates, 1.5 billion people are still affected by conflict. The rich history and legacy of peace approaches provide an indication that conflict has been addressed historically, and how new approaches are emerging.

First, the victor's peace remains relevant in policy thinking and influences conflict management approaches. Some aspects of the liberal peacebuilding and statebuilding frameworks have been criticized as such, especially in the context of Afghanistan and Iraq, as well as in the negative peace framework of conflict management applied from the 1950s to the 1970s, from Suez, to Cyprus, Congo, and the Middle East.

Secondly, the constitutional peace projects of the early Enlightenment period were a significant attempt to move beyond the cruder versions of the victor's peace, by focusing on democracy, human rights, development, and free trade. This has provided the basis for the bulk of post-Enlightenment advances in peace thinking and practices.

Similarly, the third strand of thinking about peace—an institutional peace—is now the goal of much of the UN system, and represents the main contribution of the 20th century. It has been more widely applied since the end of the Cold War. Security, governance, law, civil society, democracy, human rights, and trade, enshrined in domestic constitutional documentation, and in international treaties, have been placed at the heart of the new peace. However, it has also begun to shift into a more limited neoliberal framework for peace, which has raised concerns that this form of peace is not self-sustaining.

With the development of a fourth approach, a civil society and NGO discourse on the 'civil peace', many of the elements of the contemporary liberal peace were now present. The civil peace also draws on social theories of conflict and violence, and offers the objective of social justice. From this perspective a positive hybrid peace becomes possible.

The liberal peace, aimed at creating a liberal state (or a neoliberal state in the 2000s) as a solution to conflict, has brought much of this thinking together via peacebuilding and statebuilding approaches. Most of the international, regional, state, and civil levels, policies, and actors involved in security matters, development, and various forms of peacemaking have since followed suit. They have used it in a wide range of post-war cases across the world since the end of the Cold War.

All four components of the liberal peace—victor's, constitutional, institutional, and civil peace, as well as the first, second, and third generation approaches to peacemaking—depend upon a mix of external actors' intervention, local agency, and legitimacy. The liberal peace is depicted in Figure 9 and the first three generations of peacemaking can be summarized as in Figure 10 (see Figures 9 and 10).

The historical evolution of peace can be summarized as follows. The ancient to the medieval period saw the development of the victor's peace, wise governance to avoid war, truces and treaty

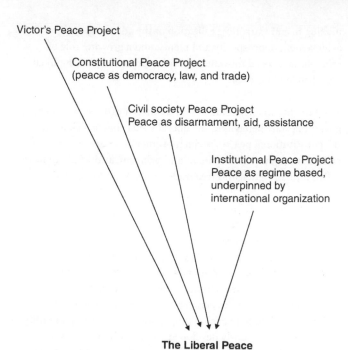

Victor's Peace Project

Constitutional Peace Project
(peace as democracy, law, and trade)

Civil society Peace Project
Peace as disarmament, aid, assistance

Institutional Peace Project
Peace as regime based,
underpinned by
international organization

**The Liberal Peace**

9. A genealogy of the liberal peace

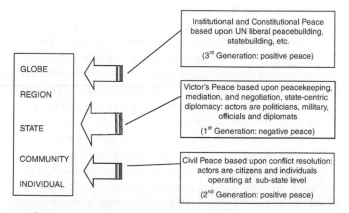

GLOBE

REGION

STATE

COMMUNITY

INDIVIDUAL

Institutional and Constitutional Peace
based upon UN liberal peacebuilding,
statebuilding, etc.

(3rd Generation: positive peace)

Victor's Peace based upon peacekeeping,
mediation, and negotiation, state-centric
diplomacy: actors are politicians, military,
officials and diplomats

(1st Generation: negative peace)

Civil Peace based upon conflict resolution:
actors are citizens and individuals
operating at sub-state level

(2nd Generation: positive peace)

10. Three generations of approaches to peacemaking

making to end wars, the realization of the advantages of achievement of prosperity and plenty, and a growing role of religious and social movements, which preached philosophical pluralism and pacifism.

The Enlightenment period added a concern with law and norms governing state behaviour, the liberal social contract (known as the constitutional peace), social movements for anti-slavery, enfranchisement, disarmament and pacifism, and what are now called human rights, and free trade.

The modern period has extended these interests into social and gender issues, as well as equality and social justice (which is known as the civil peace). It has also seen the emergence of international organizations, law, and conventions, forming an institutional peace. Other matters also emerged, including self-determination, development, and aid, and, more significantly, the democratic peace. To achieve these, humanitarian intervention, liberal peacebuilding, and neoliberal statebuilding have been most recently developed, along with processes of transitional justice, in post-conflict countries around the world.

The evolution of the main strands of thinking about peace, and the various generations of approaches to building it, have enabled major advances across a range of fields, issues, and actors. This description of the evolution of peace, which only captures its development in a limited manner, gives rise to the question of what emerges next. A fourth generation of peace thinking and practice may involve hybrid, empathetic, emancipatory notions of peace resting upon pluralism, international responses to inequality, meaning local and global redistribution, new forms of polity, the recognition of a range of everyday and transnational peace agencies, and participatory forms of democracy from the local to the global. Rather than being externally imposed it might form locally and be *enabled* in multiple ways by a range of international and local actors cooperating with each other (as with the local infrastructures for peace already mentioned). This phenomenon might indicate the emergence of a post-liberal peace in hybrid form (i.e. a positive hybrid form of peace), representing the next step in peace theory and practice, and depending on local forms of peace practice as well as international capacity and support.

An international architecture that ameliorates a wide range of issues that contribute to the creation of conflict—from poverty and inequality, to a lack of access to clean water, roads, food, markets, and public services—now exists. Its objective is to transform local conditions that give rise to conflict as well as to improve international capacity to assist in making a more sustainable peace in the context of local needs, international norms, and the global political economy. It also attempts to transform states into liberal democracies, while observing human rights and a rule of law, developing a social contract, observing the sovereignty of their regional neighbours, and enabling their entry into the globalized marketplace—with varying degrees of success.

Overall, this peace architecture has emerged as a response to past conflicts and to prevent future conflict. It has often reflected the interests and ideologies of dominant actors in the international system (meaning the West or developed global north). Even so, as this volume has illustrated, approaches to peace are developing quickly and with far-reaching effects for improving everyday lives for humanity. Its achievements have been manifold. Much more remains to be done, however.

The consequence of the rich, global, historical heritage of peace thinking and peacemaking spanning the arts to history and politics, as well as social struggles for equality outlined in this short study, are the emergence of interconnected and multiple forms of peace. These are still coming into being. They reflect hybrid variations of both the 'northern' liberal and many other localized versions of peace, influenced by many international, state, contextual, and localized dynamics.

The culmination of the developing concept of peace lies in a general recognition that the vast majority of humanity have preferred, and actively worked towards, a culture of peace. Many have worked for this selflessly throughout human history, across all fields of human knowledge, leaving an inestimable legacy upon which future generations can continue to build.

# Further reading

## Chapter 1: Defining peace

Augustine, *The City of God against the Pagans*, trans. R. W. Dyson (New York: Cambridge University Press, 1998).

Confucius, *Confucius: Analects—With Selections from Traditional Commentaries*, trans. E. Slingerland (Indianapolis: Hackett Publishing, 2003 [*c.*551–479 BC]).

Doyle, Michael, 'Kant, Liberal Legacies, and Foreign Affairs', *Philosophy and Public Affairs*, 12 (1983).

Erasmus, 'The Complaint of Peace', *The Essential Erasmus*, ed. John Dolan (New York: Continuum, 1990).

Foucault, M., 'Truth and Power', in P. Rabinow (ed.), *The Foucault Reader* (London: Penguin, 1989).

Gallie, W. B., *Philosophers of Peace and War: Kant, Clausewitz, Marx, Engels and Tolstoy* (Cambridge: Cambridge University Press, 1978).

Gandhi, Mahatma, *The Collected Works of Mahatma Gandhi* (New Delhi: Publications Division, Ministry of Information and Broadcasting, Govt. of India, 1994).

Gittings, John, *The Glorious Art of Peace* (Oxford: Oxford University Press, 2012).

Hobbes, Thomas, *Leviathan* (Oxford: Oxford University Press, 1998 [1651]).

Howard, Michael, *The Invention of Peace and War* (London: Profile Books, 2000).

Kant, Immanuel, *Perpetual Peace* (London: Allen and Unwin, 1917 [1795]).

Kelly, Raymond, *Warless Societies and the Origin of War* (Ann Arbor: University of Michigan Press, 2000).

Kissinger, H., *A World Restored: Metternich, Castlereagh and the Problems of Peace, 1812–22* (Boston: Houghton Mifflin, 1957).

Young, Nigel (ed.), *Encyclopaedia for Peace* (Oxford: Oxford University Press, 2011). <http://www.peacefulsocieties.org/>.

## Chapter 2: Peace in history

Adolf, Antony, *Peace: A World History* (Cambridge: Polity, 2009).

Cruce, Emerie, *The New Cyneas of Emerie Cruce*, trans. Thomas Willing Balch (Charleston, SC: BiblioLife, 2009 [1623]).

Erasmus, 'The Arts of Peace', in Lisa Jardine (ed.), *The Education of a Christian Prince* (Cambridge: Cambridge University Press, 1997 [1516]).

Erasmus, 'Antipolemus, or, the Plea of Reason, Religion, and Humanity against War', reprinted in *The Book of Peace: A Collection of Essays on War and Peace* (Boston: George C. Beckwith, 1845).

Fry, Douglas, *Beyond War* (Oxford: Oxford University Press, 2007).

Grotius, Hugo, *The Rights of War and Peace*, trans. A. C. Campbell (London: Dunne, 1901 [1625]).

Holt, J. C., *Magna Carta* (2nd edn. Cambridge: Cambridge University Press, 1992).

Johansen, B., *Native American Legal Tradition* (New York: Greenwood, 1998).

Kant, Immanuel, *Perpetual Peace* (London: Allen and Unwin, 1917 [1795]).

Locke, John, *A Letter Concerning Toleration, and Two Treatises on Government*, ed. Ian Shapiro (New Haven, Conn.: Yale University Press, 2003).

Marx, Karl, and Engels, Friedrich, *The Communist Manifesto* (London: Penguin, 2006 [1848]).

Penn, William, 'An Essay towards the Present and Future Peace of Europe', in *The Peace of Europe* (London: Everyman, 1993 [1693]).

Rousseau, Jean-Jacques, *The Social Contract*, ed. G. D. Cole (Thousand Oaks, Calif.: BN Publishers, 2007 [1762]).

Thoreau, Henry David, *Resistance to Civil Government* (Carlisle, Mass.: Applewood Books, 2000 [1849]).

Tolstoy, Leo, *The Kingdom of God is Within You* (Lincoln, Nebr.: Bison Books, 1984 [1894]).

# Chapter 3: Peace in modernity

Azar, E. A., *The Management of Protracted Social Conflict* (London: Dartmouth Publishing, 1990).

Bhabha, H., *The Location of Culture* (London: Routledge, 1994).

Burton, J., *World Society* (Cambridge: Cambridge University Press, 1972).

Einstein, Albert, Freud, Sigmund, and Jäckh, Ernst, *Why War? 'Open Letters' Between Einstein & Freud* (London: The New Commonwealth. A society for the promotion of international law and order, 1934).

Fanon, F., *The Wretched of the Earth*, trans. Constance Farrington (New York: Grove Weidenfeld, 1963 [1961]).

Foucault, M., *The Birth of Politics*, trans. Graham Burchell (London: Palgrave, 2009).

Freire, P., *Pedagogy of the Oppressed* (London: Penguin, 1996 [1970]).

Hochschild, Adam, *Bury the Chains* (London: Macmillan, 2005).

Keynes, J. M., *The Economic Consequences of the Peace* (London: Macmillan, 1920).

International Commission on Intervention and State Sovereignty (ICISS), *Responsibility to Protect* (Ottawa: International Development Research Centre, December 2001).

Mitrany, D. A., *The Functional Theory of Politics* (London: Martin Robertson, 1975).

Richmond, Oliver P., *Maintaining Order, Making Peace* (London: Palgrave, 2002).

Richmond, Oliver P., *The Transformation of Peace* (London: Palgrave, 2005).

Russell, Bertrand, *The Collected Papers of Bertrand Russell*, xiv: *Pacifism and Revolution 1916–18* (London: Unwin Hyman, 1995).

Scott, J. C., *Domination and the Arts of Resistance* (New Haven, Conn.: Yale University Press, 1990).

Sen, Amartya, *Development as Freedom* (Oxford: Oxford University Press, 1999).

Tuck, Richard, *The Rights of War and Peace* (Oxford: Oxford University Press, 1999).

UNDP, *Human Development Report* (New York: UNDP, 1994).

Walzer, Michael, *Just and Unjust Wars: A Moral Argument with Historical Illustrations* (4th edn. New York: Basic Books, 1977).

Weber, Max, *The Vocation Lectures* (Indianapolis: Hackett, 2004 [1919]).

## Chapter 4: The victors' peace in history

Galtung, J., 'Violence, Peace, and Peace Research', *Journal of Peace Research*, 6:3 (1969).

Hammarskjold, Dag, *Summary Study*, UN doc. A/3943, 9 October 1958.

Hegel, G. W. F., *Philosophy of Right* (London: Prometheus, 1996).

Hobbes, Thomas, *Leviathan* (Oxford: Oxford University Press, 1998 [1651]).

Keynes, J. M., *The Economic Consequences of the Peace* (London: Macmillan, 1920).

Kissinger, Henry, *A World Restored: Metternich, Castlereagh and the Problems of Peace, 1812-22* (Boston: Houghton Mifflin, 1957).

Machiavelli, Niccolò, *The Prince*, trans. Harvey Mansfield (Chicago: University of Chicago Press, 1985).

Princen, Thomas, *Intermediaries in International Conflict* (Princeton: Princeton University Press, 1992).

Sherman, W. H., *John Dee: The Politics of History in the English Renaissance* (Amherst: Massachusetts University Press, 1995).

Sun Tzu, *The Art of War*, trans. John Minford (New York: Viking, 2002).

Thucydides, *The Peloponnesian War*, trans. Steven Lattimore (Indianapolis: Hackett, 1998).

Vitoria, Francisco, *The Law of War on the Indians*, trans. Ernest Nys (London: Oceana Publications Inc., 1964 [1532]).

## Chapter 5: The constitutional peace

Bentham, J., *The Collected Works* (Oxford: Clarendon, 1996 [1839]).

Ceadel, Martin, *Thinking About Peace and War* (Oxford: Oxford University Press, 1987).

Doyle, Michael, 'Kant, Liberal Legacies, and Foreign Affairs', *Philosophy and Public Affairs*, 12 (1983).

Gittings, John, *The Glorious Art of Peace* (Oxford: Oxford University Press, 2012).

Kant, Immanuel, *Perpetual Peace* (London: Allen and Unwin, 1917 [1795]).

Locke, John, *A Letter Concerning Toleration*, and *Two Treaties on Government*, ed. Ian Shapiro (New Haven, Conn.: Yale University Press, 2003).

Mill, John Stuart, *On Liberty* (Oxford: Oxford University Press, 1998 [1859]).

Mill, John Stuart, *Principles of Political Economy* (Oxford: Oxford University Press, 2010 [1848]).

Paris, Roland, and Sisk, Timothy, *The Dilemmas of Statebuilding* (London: Routledge, 2008).

Ricardo, David, *On the Principles of Political Economy and Taxation* (Amherst, Mass.: Prometheus Books, 1996 [1821]).

Roberts, Adam, and Kingsbury, Benedict (eds.), *United Nations, Divided World* (2nd edn. London: Oxford University Press, 1996).

Smith, Adam, *An Inquiry into the Nature and Causes of the Wealth of Nations* (Chicago: University of Chicago Press; Facsimile of 1904 edition, 1977 [1776]).

## Chapter 6: The institutional peace

Barash, David, *Approaches to Peace* (Oxford: Oxford University Press, 2000).

Brown, Chris, *International Relations Theory* (London: Harvester Wheatsheaf, 1992).

Brownlie, Ian, *Principles of Public International Law* (Oxford: Oxford University Press, 2008).

Carr, E. H., *The Twenty Years Crisis* (London: Macmillan, 1939).

Fanon, F., *The Wretched of the Earth*, trans. Constance Farrington (New York: Grove Weidenfeld, [1961] 1963).

*Geneva Conventions*, 1864, 1949, and *Additional Protocols*, 1977.

Gittings, John, *The Glorious Art of Peace* (Oxford: Oxford University Press, 2012).

Ikenberry, G. John, *After Victory* (Princeton: Princeton University Press, 2001).

'International Covenant on Economic, Social and Cultural Rights', *General Assembly Resolution 2200A (XXI)*, 16 December 1966 (entered into force 3 January 1976, in accordance with article 27).

Keynes, John Maynard, *The Economic Consequences of the Peace* (London: Macmillan, 1920).

Link, Arthur S., et al. (eds.), *The Papers of Woodrow Wilson*, xli: *January 24–April 6, 1917* (Princeton: Princeton University Press, 1983).

Macmillan, Margaret, *The Peacemakers* (London: John Murray, 2003).

Mitrany, David, *The Functional Theory of Politics* (London: Martin Robertson, 1975).

Owen, Nicolas (ed.), *Human Rights, Human Wrongs* (Oxford: Oxford University Press, 2002).

Penn, William, 'An Essay towards the Present and Future Peace of Europe', in *The Peace of Europe* (London: Everyman, 1993 [1693]).

Rieff, David, *A Bed for the Night* (London: Vintage, 2002).

Saint-Pierre, Abbé de, *A Project for Settling an Everlasting Peace in Europe, 1714–1738* (London, 1714).

Steel, R., *Walter Lippmann and the American Century* (Boston: Little Brown and Company, 1980).

Taylor, Paul, and Groom, A. J. R. (eds.), *The UN at the Millennium* (London: Continuum, 2000).

Williams, Andrew, *Failed Imagination: New World Orders of the Twentieth Century* (Manchester: Manchester University Press, 1998).

## Chapter 7: The civil peace

Anderson, Mary B., *Do No Harm* (Boulder, Colo.: Lynne Rienner Publishers, 1999).

Azar, E. A., *The Management of Protracted Social Conflict* (London: Dartmouth Publishing, 1990).

Barash, David, *Approaches to Peace* (Oxford: Oxford University Press, 2000).

Boulding, Elise, *Cultures of Peace* (Syracuse, NY: Syracuse University Press, 2000).

Josselin, Daphne, and Wallace, William (eds.), *Non-State Actors in World Politics* (London: Palgrave, 2001).

Keane, John, *Global Civil Society?* (Cambridge: Cambridge University Press, 2003).

Keck, Margeret E., and Sikkind, Kathryn, *Activists Beyond Borders* (Ithaca, NY: Cornell University Press, 1998).

Mendlovitz, S., and Walker, R. B. J. (eds.), *Towards a Just World Peace* (London: Butterworths, 1987).

Ramsbotham, Oliver, and Woodhouse, Tom, *Humanitarian Intervention in Contemporary Conflict* (Cambridge: Polity Press, 2005).

Tadjbakhsh, Sharhbanou, and Chenoy, Anuradha M., *Human Security: Concepts and Implications* (London: Routledge, 2006).

UNDP, *Human Development Report* (New York: UNDP, 2002).

Willets, Peter, 'From "Consultative Arrangements" to "Partnership": The Changing Status of NGOs in Diplomacy at the UN', *Global Governance*, 6 (2000).

# Chapter 8: Peacekeeping, peacebuilding, and statebuilding

Bellamy, Alex, and Williams, Paul, 'Peace Operations and Global Order', *International Peacekeeping*, 10:4 (2004).

Bercovitch, J. (ed.), *Resolving International Conflicts: The Theory and Practice of Mediation* (London: Boulder, 1996).

Boutros-Ghali, Boutros, *An Agenda for Peace: Preventative Diplomacy, Peacemaking and Peacekeeping* (New York: United Nations, 1992).

*Busan Partnership for Effective Development Co-operation. Fourth High Level Forum on Aid Effectiveness* (Busan, Republic of Korea, 29 November–1 December 2011).

Call, Charles T., and Cook, Susan E., 'On Democratisation and Peacebuilding', *Global Governance*, 9:2 (2003).

Cousens, Elizabeth, and Kumar, C., *Peacebuilding as Politics* (Boulder, Colo.: Lynne Rienner, 2001).

*European Security Strategy* (2003).

Fukuyama, Francis, *State Building: Governance and Order in the Twenty First Century* (London: Profile, 2004).

International Commission on Intervention, *The Responsibility to Protect: The Report of the International Commission on Intervention and State Sovereignty* (Ottawa: International Development Research Centre, 2002).

Kapur, D., 'The State in a Changing World: A Critique of the 1997 World Development Report', *WCFIA Working Paper No. 98-02* (1998).

Lederach, Jean Paul, *Building Peace* (Washington, DC: United States Institute of Peace, 1997).

Lund, Michael S., *Preventing Violent Conflicts* (Washington, DC: USIP, 1996).

Miall, Hugh, *Conflict Transformation: A Multi-Dimensional Task* (Berghof Handbook for Conflict Transformation, 2004).

OECD-DAC, *Principles for Good International Engagement in Fragile States* (2005).

*Peacebuilding & The United Nations* (United Nations Peacebuilding Support Office, United Nations, 2012).

Ponzio, Richard, *Democratic Peacebuilding* (Oxford: Oxford University Press, 2011).

Pouligny, Beatrice, *Peace Operations Seen from Below* (London: Hurst, 2006).

Pugh, Michael, Cooper, Neil, and Turner, Mandy (eds.), *Whose Peace? Critical Perspectives on the Political Economy of Peacebuilding* (London: Palgrave, 2009).

Richmond, Oliver P., 'UN Peace Operations and the Dilemmas of the Peacebuilding Consensus', *International Peacekeeping*, 10:4 (2004).

Richmond, Oliver P., and Franks, Jason, 'Introduction', in *Liberal Peace Transitions: Between Statebuilding and Peacebuilding* (Edinburgh: Edinburgh University Press, 2009).

Schmid, Herman, 'Peace Research and Politics', *Journal of Peace Research*, 5:3 (1968).

UN General Assembly Resolution 60/180 (20 December 2005).

UN Secretary Report on 'Peacebuilding in the Immediate Aftermath of Conflict', A/63/881 (11 June 2009).

UNDP, *Development Report* (1994).

*US National Security Strategy* (2002).

Wilkinson, Richard, and Pickett, Kate, *The Spirit Level: Why Equality Is Better for Everyone* (London: Penguin, 2009).

World Bank, *The State in a Changing World* (Washington, DC: World Bank, 1997).

Zartman, I. William, *Ripe for Resolution* (Oxford: For the Council of Foreign Relations, 1989).

## Chapter 9: Hybrid forms of peace

Alden, C., 'The United Nations and Demilitarisation in Mozambique', *International Peacekeeping*, 2:2 (1995).

Boege, Volker, Brown, Anne, Clements, Kevin P., and Nolan, Anna, 'States Emerging from Hybrid Political Orders—Pacific Experiences', *The Australian Centre for Peace and Conflict Studies (ACPACS) Occasional Papers Series* (2008).

Brown, Anne, *Security and Development in the Pacific Islands* (Boulder, Colo.: Lynne Rienner, 2007).

Chambers, R., *Rural Development: Putting the Last First* (London: Longman, 1983).

G7+, *Dili Declaration*, April 2010: 'Busan Partnership for Effective Development Co-operation', *Fourth High Level Forum On Aid Effectiveness* (Busan, Republic of Korea, 29 November–1 December 2011).

Hadjipavlou, M., 'The Cyprus Conflict: Root Causes and Implications for Peacebuilding', *Journal of Peace Research*, 44:3 (2007).

Hayman, C., 'Ripples into Waves: Locally Led Peacebuilding on a National Scale' (Peace Direct/Quakers UN Office, 2010).

Ihsanoglu, E., Allen Nan, Susan, Cherian Mampilly, Zachariah, and Bartoli, Andrea, *Peacemaking: From Practice to Theory* (Westport, Conn.: Praeger, 2011).

Johnson, P., *Local vs. National Peacebuilding: The Richness of Somali Peacemaking*, <http://www.prio.no/peaceethics/PeacE-Discussions> (2010).

Jonas, Susanne, *Of Centaurs and Doves: Guatemala's Peace Process* (Boulder, Colo.: Westview Press, 2000).

Kemp, Graham, and Fry, Douglas P., *Keeping the Peace: Peaceful Societies Around the World* (London: Routledge, 2004).

Lister, Sarah, 'Understanding State-Building and Local Government in Afghanistan', *Crisis States Research Centre Working Paper No. 14* (May 2007).

Pouligny, B., *Peace Operations Seen from Below* (London: Hurst, 2006).

Pouligny, B., *Supporting Local Ownership in Humanitarian Action*, Humanitarian Policy Paper Series (Berlin: Global Public Policy Institute, 2009).

Richmond, Oliver P., *A Post-Liberal Peace* (London: Routledge, 2011).

Roberts, Adam, and Garton Ash, Timothy (eds.), *Civil Resistance and Power Politics* (Oxford: Oxford University Press, 2009).

Tilly, C., *Democracy* (Cambridge: Cambridge University Press, 2007).

UNDP, *Governance for Peace* (New York, 2012).

UNESCO Culture of Peace Programme in El Salvador (1992).

UN Secretary General Report on 'Peacebuilding in the Immediate Aftermath of Conflict', *A/63/881* (11 June 2009).

World Bank, *Issues and Options for Improving Engagement between the World Bank and Civil Society Organisations* (Washington, DC, 2005).

Wyeth, V., 'Knights in Fragile Armour: The Rise of the G7+', *Global Governance*, 18 (2011).

# Index

Peace